The U.S. Marine Corps in Crisis

Keith Fleming

The U.S. Marine Corps in Crisis

Ribbon Creek and Recruit Training

University of South Carolina Press

Copyright © University of South Carolina 1990

Published in Columbia, South Carolina, by the
University of South Carolina Press

Manufactured in the United States of America

First Edition

Library of Congress Cataloging-in-Publication Data

Fleming, Keith, 1941–
    The U.S. Marine Corps in crisis: Ribbon Creek and recruit
training / Keith Fleming
        p. cm.
    Includes bibliographical references.
    ISBN 0-87249-635-X
    1. Military education—United States—Basic training—
History—20th century. 2. United States. Marine Corps—
History—20th century. I. Title.
VE432.F54 1989
359.9'6'0973—dc20   89-38175
                                                      CIP

For
Kathryn, Joanna, and John

Contents

List of Illustrations   viii

Author's Note   ix

Preface   xi

Acknowledgments   xiii

Acronyms and Abbreviations   xv

Introduction   1

1. Development of the Maltreatment Problem   10
2. The Ribbon Creek Incident   29
3. The Immediate Reaction   40
4. Instituting the Changes   56
5. The McKeon Court-Martial   74
6. Making the Changes Work   87
7. Greene's Downfall   101
8. Postscript   111

Notes   122

Bibliography   139

Index   145

List of Illustrations

Following page 46

1. Aerial photo of rifle range
2. General Randolph Pate
3. General Wallace Greene
4. General Shoup inspecting honor guard with General Greene
5. General Greene removing rank insignia
6. Attorney Berman and Sergeant McKeon
7. School Building and site of court-martial
8. Recruits practicing bayonet training

Author's Note

Even though I am employed as a civilian historian for the U.S. Marine Corps, the research and writing of this book, like that for the dissertation from which it derives, were done on my own time. This history should not be construed as representing the official policies or position of the U.S. Department of Defense, the U.S. Department of the Navy, or the U.S. Marine Corps. The opinions and conclusions expressed herein are my own, as are any errors or omissions.

Keith Fleming
Woodbridge, Virginia
July 16, 1988

Preface

This book, in a certain sense, is not about the Ribbon Creek incident at Parris Island, South Carolina, in 1956; it is about the United States at midcentury. From that perspective, Ribbon Creek is simply a lens through which we can examine some facets of American culture in an era now thirty years in the past.

The United States was under a great deal of stress in the mid-1950s. One source of that stress was fear for the nation's security. The post-World War II reliance on nuclear weapons as the relatively inexpensive key to national defense had not prevented the conventional war in Korea. The country's conventional forces, particularly its ground combat forces, had not been kept ready for such a war. Their initial introduction into combat in Korea almost resulted in total defeat due to five years of post-World War II national neglect. Throughout the war in Korea, newly arrived American combat troops had trouble at first in negotiating the Korean mountains on foot. Americans worried about the stamina and physical fitness of the younger generation and found Communist propaganda about decadent American society unsettling. Post-Korean War revelations about "collaboration" by American prisoners of war added to the discomfiture.

The armistice that ended the fighting in Korea did not bring an and to these worries. It also did not end the problems and the debate regarding national security. Nuclear weapons were not the answer to all questions of national defense; Korea proved the United States would have to abandon a historic practice and maintain strong conventional forces in peacetime. This meant, in that era, a peacetime draft and a stint of military service for about 75 percent of young Americans of military age. Military service, in effect, became part of growing up in America. Those with college deferments were as much a part of the phenomenon as those drafted after graduation from high school. Unable to escape the obligation to serve, many enlisted in the service of their choice rather than trust to the uncertainty of the draft. In either case, they were considered to be making a patriotic sacrifice of some years of their lives.

There was, nevertheless, a dichotomy in the way the nation viewed its sons' military training. The nation did not want a repetition of the problems in training encountered early in the Korean War. It wanted its combat men well trained and ready. On the other hand, America wanted its sons treated with the respect and admiration their patriotic sacrifice deserved.

Finding a middle ground between these two imperatives was not easy for the Armed Services. They also faced their own internal problems of adapting to a new peacetime size and role. They did adapt in time and, in the process, shaped the modern American military system.

The military's adaptation was not an easy or a smooth path. Sometimes it was rough going; sometimes there was tragedy. This book derives from one of the latter, but the incident itself serves primarily as a vehicle for examining larger issues. The first of these is the external stresses upon the corporate body of Marine noncommissioned officers during the early Cold War, and how those stresses affected their corporate outlook and behavior. The second is the Marine Corps' relationship to the U.S. Congress in the 1950s. The third issue centers on the complex nature of the justice system in America, and how public opinion can play a role in the ultimate outcome. Finally, this book gives an example of the mechanics and difficulty of institutional reform. These issues cut across several scholarly disciplines and illustrate that military history involves more than battle narratives.

As an undergraduate, I took several courses from a pioneering southeastern archaeologist, David L. DeJarnette. In discussing categories of artifacts, he said those who establish the categories tend to fall into two groups: "lumpers" and "splitters." The former wanted to lump as many artifacts as possible into a single type; the latter separated them based upon the slightest differences.

When it comes to discussing types of historical subdisciplines, I am a lumper. In this volume on the Ribbon Creek incident, military, political, and social history intertwine. There is no need to separate them; they are shoots from the same vine.

Acknowledgments

My thanks go to Dr. Allan R. Millett for his encouragement of the completion of this project. His support was constant through both the earlier dissertation and its conversion into book form.

I am particularly grateful to my former colleagues on the staff of the Marine Corps Historical Center in Washington, D.C. Brigadier General Edwin H. Simmons, USMC (Ret.) brought the Historical Center into being and created the policies that ease scholarly research into Marine Corps records. In addition, he has my appreciation for the many tutorials on the elements of good writing. Mrs. Joyce E. Bonnett, the head of the Archives Section, was always helpful in locating records in her immediate holdings and in bringing Marine Corps records from the National Records Center, Suitland, Maryland. Mr. Charles A. Wood, formerly the head of the Personal Papers Section and now chief curator of the Marine Corps Museum, guided me through the voluminous papers of retired General Wallace M. Greene, Jr., and also made arrangements to have boxes of papers available during nonworking hours. Mr. J. Michael Miller, who succeeded Mr. Wood in the section, continued that support. Mr. Benis M. Frank, head of the Oral History Section, steered me toward the most fruitful interviews. Mr. Danny J. Crawford and his Reference Section staff invariably took time to aid my search through the Historical Center's extensive reference files. Mrs. Regina Strother was a source of good advice on photographs from the Ribbon Creek period. The head librarian, Miss Evelyn A. Englander, and her assistant, Mrs. Patricia E. Morgan, cheerfully helped me find the needed published sources, whether from the stacks or through interlibrary loan. They also spent over eight years providing me with good books to read and study. Colonel James R. Williams, head of the Historical Branch; Mr. Henry I. Shaw, Jr., the chief historian, and Mr. Jack Shulimson, head of the Histories

Section, were supportive and encouraged my writing. Mr. Shaw's candid advice on the nature of the Marine Corps and the details of its history were invaluable. Mr. Jack Shulimson, who is also the Historical Center's senior Vietnam historian and a valued friend, helped immeasurably by debating my developing ideas.

Four retired Marine general officers—General Wallace M. Greene, Jr., General Merrill H. Twining, Lieutenant General Henry W. Buse, Jr., and Brigadier General Samuel R. Shaw—generously provided answers to my many questions about the Ribbon Creek period. All four gave written comments on earlier draft chapters, which enriched the final product.

My family's support was crucial in this project. My two children, Joanna and John, reached their high school years while helping their parents through two doctorates. They have gone off to college while awaiting and encouraging the completion of this book. It has been their effort, too. My wife, Kathryn, has been a magnificent source of strength and love throughout. She has her own professional career, but has supported this project while shouldering more than her share of parental and family responsibilities. She has my admiration as well as my love.

I could not have completed this history without the help of those listed above; however, I bear sole responsibility for any errors.

Acronyms and Abbreviations

AC/S	Assistant Chief of Staff
AP	Associated Press
BOQ	bachelor officers quarters
CG	Commanding General
CMC	Commandant of the Marine Corps
DI	drill instructor
GCT	General Classification Test
HQMC	Headquarters Marine Corps
IG	inspector general
INS	International News Service
MCB	Marine Corps Base
MCRD	Marine Corps Recruit Depot
NCO	noncommissioned officer
PFC	private first class
PT	physical training
RTC	Recruit Training Command
SOP	Standing operating procedures
UCMJ	Uniform Code of Military Justice
USMC	United States Marine Corps
USMCR	United States Marine Corps Reserve

The U.S. Marine
Corps in Crisis

Introduction

On a Sunday evening in April 1956, a U.S. Marine Corps drill instructor led his recruit platoon into Ribbon Creek, a tidal stream at Parris Island, South Carolina. Six men drowned, setting off a furor among both defenders and detractors of Marine Corps training methods. However, even before it published the first news release on the Ribbon Creek tragedy, the Corps already had taken the first steps in a process that eventually contained the situation by heading off a congressional investigation, preserved the fundamental nature of Marine recruit training, and rendered the furor, including that portion emanating from the Corps' supporters, an irrelevant nuisance. The Corps achieved its goals by hammering out a consensus within its own leadership and with Congress for selective and limited reforms designed to eliminate abuses in recruit training. Only then did it announce its reform plans.

This scenario was not the only option open to the Marine Corps. In the jargon of the Watergate affair of the 1970s, the Corps could have "stonewalled" and strongly resisted any changes on the grounds that, in the midst of the Cold War, it was folly to alter a system that had molded the Marines who had won so many battles in World War II and Korea. This option, however, would have had little chance of success, despite the political clout that had helped the Marines get their force structure written into law only four years earlier. In 1956 the Corps was on weak ground because it knew that the Ribbon Creek tragedy was symptomatic of wider recruit training problems likely to be exposed by a congressional investigation. In addition, it would have been political folly to have alienated Congress during the years of the Eisenhower administration's "New Look" defense policy, which instituted manpower and procurement cuts in conventional forces such as the Marine Corps in favor of the less costly nuclear deterrent.

1

At the other end of the spectrum was the option of a total overhaul of the Corps' recruit training system to bring it in line with the other Armed Services. Few of the Marines' advocates would have supported such a move. The Cold War made combat appear possible at any time, and a new recruit training system might adversely affect combat readiness. Many Marines, in addition, believed that the major lesson of the Korean War was that poorly trained, poorly disciplined troops do not win battles. Further, both the American public and the Marines still expected toughness in Marine training.

The Marine Corps wisely opted for the middle ground that would allow it to set its own house in order without a congressional investigation. The first step, as in most reforms, was a housecleaning to put whole new management teams in charge of the training bases. Additional numbers of commissioned officers went to the recruit depots to provide increased supervision of the enlisted drill instructors.

To ensure that this loss of their traditional automomy would not create an adverse reaction among the drill instructors (DIs), the depots took action to increase the DIs' perquisites and prestige. Among these actions was a revival of the old pre-World War II campaign hat as the DIs' badge of office, a larger allowance of uniforms, coupled with free laundry to enhance personal appearance, and the provision of better living quarters for both bachelor and married DIs.

Efforts to toughen the training took several forms. First, the length of the training increased by two weeks. Second, a new emphasis on physical training added to the image of a more rugged program and, at the same time, brought the Corps in line with a national concern for youth physical fitness. It also corrected one of the major complaints of the Corps' combat arm, the Fleet Marine Force. Graduates from recruit training all too often were not physically prepared for the rigors of advanced infantry training.[1]

The Marine response to Ribbon Creek also included what could be described as "social programs." A newly created special unit had the task of handling overweight, weak, and unmotivated recruits who otherwise would not complete recruit training. This reduced the pressures on drill instructors by removing problem cases from the regular recruit platoons. The new Special Training Branch gave its charges the individual attention needed either to correct their deficiencies and return to normal training or to process them for discharge from the service.

The final major element in the response was a vigorous public relations effort, primarily by the Marine generals at Parris Island, in keeping with the Marine policy of decentralization of public relations. Both depots widely advertised an "open door" policy in which anyone—individuals or groups—were welcome to come at any time to see Marine recruit training. The campaign at Parris Island paid special attention to the eastern cities in which the local news media had carried stories critical of the Marine Corps. Parris Island, in coordination with Marine recruiters in these cities, invited groups of civic and business leaders to fly to the depot in Marine aircraft for four-to-five day orientation visits, all at the Corps' expense. These groups, as well as the working press, received carefully orchestrated tours and public relations material highlighting the value and improvements to the recruit training program.

These reform measures, though extensive, were primarily administrative, and none touched the "shock treatment" that formed the fundamental element of Marine recruit training. The shock treatment involved an abrupt and stressful change from the civilian world to that of a Marine recruit. The Corps first removed the visible symbols of a recruit's civilian status and individuality: his clothing and hairstyle. Short-haired and dressed in a wrinkled new uniform, each recruit, regardless of background, began his military service on an equal basis with his contemporaries. A hectic schedule in unfamiliar surroundings; shouting, cursing drill instructors who quickly destroyed one's civilian concept of self-worth by violating one's personal space with face-to-face, nose-to-nose harangues; this, coupled with exhaustion, completed a recruit's disorientation. Most human beings, however, are adaptable. The new recruits quickly learned the new social rules. With no other role models than their drill instructors, the recruits identified with their new leaders and tried to imitate them to become Marines.[2]

This process theoretically served to turn civilians into "basic Marines," not combat-ready infantrymen. Training for the latter came afterward when all recruit graduates went on to further training at an Infantry Training Regiment, followed by other specialized training, as required.

The recruit depots' only involvement in combat training in 1956 was in conducting the recruit program so as to test the new men in an intense, high-stress environment. Even today DIs say that it is better to have a man break in recruit training rather than in combat where he could get other Marines killed.[3]

Marines believed in the value of their recruit training, commonly called "boot camp," but by the mid-1950s it had become notorious for hazing and maltreatment of its trainees. The two terms, "hazing" and "maltreatment," are difficult to define precisely in the recruit-training context and, in Marine jargon, "maltreatment" usually covers both terms. Every Marine has his definition of maltreatment, and even the official definition has varied through time. For example, official restrictions on drill instructors' use of profanity have tended to become more rigid as a means of preventing the degrading of recruits. In the post-Ribbon Creek period, the list of prohibited acts considered to be hazing included, among others: duck walking, hiking with packs full of sand, dry shaving while running in place (often with a bucket over the recruit's head), and using locker boxes as barbells. The list totaled twenty-two items defined under the category of hazing. The maltreatment category contained twenty-nine items, including punching recruits in the stomach, burning recruits with cigarettes, forcing recruits to eat cigarettes, stacking recruits in trash bins, refusing to allow recruits to use insect repellent or making recruits run the "belt line," a gauntlet of belt-swinging fellow recruits. In general, the Marine Corps has defined maltreatment as any practice that degrades the individual or causes him pain or injury.[4]

The reasons for maltreatment are complex and go beyond the recruit depots to encompass the whole Marine Corps of the 1950s. Part of the maltreatment problem lies with the long-standing Marine assumption that discipline, as exemplified by immediate obedience to orders, was the overriding factor in combat success. This belief created a reliance upon noncommissioned officer (NCO) leadership based upon domination. The problem with this form of leadership in the 1950s was that American society, including the military establishment, was shifting toward more persuasive forms of leadership, which took morale and human relations into consideration.

Marine NCOs resisted this trend because they perceived it as a threat to their traditional authority and prestige. Several factors, however, including the newly instituted Uniform Code of Military Justice (UCMJ), Marine regulations, and the realities of active service constrained their reaction. The result was a high level of frustration within the NCO ranks.

These stresses upon the corporate NCO body came at a time when other stresses were also creating turmoil. World War II and then Korea left the Marine Corps with more NCOs than it needed.

Some were former temporary officers forced to revert to their permanent ranks. The excess of NCOs meant few promotions and further frustration.

The weight of these manifold stresses inevitably made itself felt at the recruit depots, for *only* there did NCOs retain what they perceived as their traditional authority. *Only* at the recruit depots could the corporate body of NCOs, acting through the drill instructors, counter the perceived crisis in discipline in the Corps. *Only* there could they have a primary role in shaping the nature of the Corps and the Marines in it, and thereby restore the prestige of the NCO.

Drill instructors, as representatives of the NCOs' corporate body, bore down on their recruits in the belief that a good, swift kick in the rear—and other forms of corporal punishment—were aids in teaching proper discipline. In the process, drill instructors narrowed their group definition of maltreatment. They condoned all practices that did not cause a recruit to bleed or require hospitalization. Drill instructors vigorously protected each other as long as this rule was not violated.[5]

One way to appreciate the maltreatment phenomenon and the stresses upon the corporate NCO body is to compare it to the reaction of another culture to stress. An illustrative example is the comparative study of two Australian aboriginal groups by anthropologist John Greenway.[6] One of the groups, the Aranda, lived in a harsh environment away from the coast. Life was precarious; the group's survival was always in doubt. Under these conditions, the Aranda developed strenuous male puberty rites, which lasted for weeks and culminated in the slicing open of the youth's penis. Other similar aboriginal groups, living in more favored environments near the coast, had initiation rites of far less severity. Their rites lasted only a few days and ended with the mere knocking out of a tooth.

There was a practical reason for the severity of the Aranda rite of passage. The precarious nature of their life demanded that the group's young men remember all they had been taught in the initiation into manhood; otherwise, they and the larger society might not survive. The Aranda male initiation ceremonies achieved that goal. "If an act is unforgettable," commented Peter Farb, "then whatever is associated with that act is unforgettable also."[7]

Most Marines considered their boot-camp experiences unforgettable; most believed the system worked. At one time I would have agreed wholeheartedly with the latter assessment. Now I am ambivalent about the stress upon discipline and immediate obedience to orders. The traditional assessment contradicts considerable social research—and my own experience—that unit cohesiveness is far more important to combat success. Men fight on the battlefield for the preservation of a small, cohesive primary group rather than any "discipline" learned in recruit or later training. In fact, overemphasis on instant, unthinking obedience to orders is counterproductive even in peacetime, since it tends to stifle initiative and the development of leadership skills among the junior ranks.[8]

Some may be surprised at my ambivalence, since I went through the Marine Corps training system and remain proud of my service as a Marine. Becoming a Marine was an ambition going back, as it did for many of my contemporaries, to a youthful exposure to John Wayne's movie, *Sands of Iwo Jima*. My Marine Corps service began immediately after high school graduation in 1959. It was a short stint. The rifle-range portion of our platoon's training was behind us, and recruit graduation was only a couple of weeks away when I dislocated my shoulder lifting barbells during physical training. The weights were not very heavy, and the doctors soon discovered I had an old shoulder injury from high school football. That earned me a quick medical discharge.

My goal to become a Marine remained. My family paid to have the problem surgically corrected. After waiting the required six months, I sought reenlistment. A recruiter helped me get my IV–F draft classification changed, and the Marine Corps gave me a waiver, which allowed me to sign up again. I returned to Parris Island in May 1960, went through the entire training program, and received a meritorious promotion to private first class (PFC) upon graduation. In retrospect, the promotion probably was inevitable, for I suspect my drill instructors had decided that anyone who wanted to be in their Marine Corps *that* much deserved a PFC stripe.

I was, indeed, a "true believer." For that reason, I must say that upon graduation from Parris Island in 1960, I too accepted the importance of "discipline" as an article of faith. Even my later experience as a commissioned officer commanding a rifle company in Vietnam seemed to support the primacy of discipline and instant obedience to orders. I carried that belief with me to my post-Vietnam assignment with the Recruit Training Regiment at San Diego, California. In general, the young Marines of that era did not seem as well trained and well disciplined as those with whom I landed in the Dominican Republic in 1965 as a rifle-platoon commander.

I was wrong. The Marines with whom I served in the Dominican Republic made up an effective unit because of cohesiveness developed over months of training together at Camp Lejeune, North Carolina. True, our initial reaction to sniper fire was to expend large amounts of ammunition, as units almost invariably do when first exposed to combat. Our cohesion fully solidified after the death of Private First Class Michael Feher, our first and only casualty. Afterward, the platoon settled down to the business of killing snipers with minimum but deadly return fire. We developed a closeness that made the fire teams and squads fight well because it was the best way to protect each other. As was generally true of the whole battalion, the unit's members looked after each other so well that no one got into trouble with the law when we later went on liberty in San Juan, Puerto Rico.

I did not encounter that level of cohesion in the 1st Marine Division in Vietnam. At the time I believed the problem could be traced to a decline in aggressive, small-unit leadership. Now I would say the real reason lay in the constant turnover of people, partly from casualties but primarily because of the loss of those rotating home. Another major factor was the "mixmaster" program, which shifted people from one unit to another to prevent excessive numbers from rotating home from a single unit at the same time.

This lessening of cohesion was not the Marine experience in World War II. The nature of the island-hopping-campaign, with its brief, intense periods of combat followed by refitting and training in rear areas, fostered the integration of replacements into primary groups because it occurred away from the actual fighting. Further, it provided the veterans a chance to pass on their experience, to train the replacements before going back into combat. Only the battles of the last year of World War II lasted long enough for the integration of replacements in the midst of combat to become a problem in Marine units.

Marines drew the wrong lesson about replacements from those last battles of World War II, as illustrated by a veteran's letter to his younger brother during the latter's recruit training at Parris Island in October 1950. The former Marine sergeant described an incident on

Saipan where a number of new replacements died needlessly because they ran when first exposed to enemy fire. The veteran continued:

> Later the oldtimers agreed that perhaps the thirty or forty days aboard ship without discipline had so loosened the claim of authority on the recruits that even when their lives depended upon it, they couldn't obey a command.
>
> I think maybe the fault lay back in Boot Camp. Maybe the DI didn't ride those lads quite hard enough. . . . learn to obey orders. Learn to do it as instinctively as you bat your eye. You'll live longer if you do.[9]

Lack of discipline had little to do with the reaction of these Saipan replacements to their first exposure to enemy fire. They acted in a perfectly normal way for men who had not been integrated into their new units. S. L. A. Marshall noted that the first exposure to combat causes intense feelings of fear, isolation, and confusion. Further, men are inherently unwilling to risk danger on behalf of people with whom they have no social identity.* Under these circumstances, a soldier has no reason to fear losing "the one thing he is likely to value more highly than his life—his reputation as a man among men."[10]

The U.S. Army studied such problems during and after World War II. The Marine Corps, particularly the NCOs, believed that tighter discipline during training would prevent such problems.

The second half of the Korean War, the period of static positions, tested the Marine belief in discipline. The introduction of the rotation system created a constant turnover of people. This, and the spatial dispersion inherent in trench systems, worked against the development and maintenance of group ties. Primary groups degenerated into a buddy relationship of two men.[11]

Marines looked to themselves for a practical solution to the problems of combat efficiency facing them during that period of the Korean War. Thorough pre-combat training could compensate somewhat for the problems of maintaining combat efficiency and integrating replacements into units even though the nature of the war in Korea had reduced primary groups and unit cohesion to a minimal level.

---

* A counterargument can point to those occasions when people have risked their lives to save absolute strangers. This, however, is the ideal, not the norm of human behavior. If it were routine, normal behavior—in essence, unremarkable—there would be no heroism awards for such acts.

An emphasis on pre-combat training fitted well with traditional Marine beliefs. Since Marines traced combat effectiveness back to discipline, they also traced it back to boot camp, the place a Marine first learns about military discipline. Edwin McDowell, in his novel about Parris Island during the Korean War, has a DI, Technical Sergeant Krupe, state this belief to a junior DI, Corporal Sanders: "Discipline is what makes Marines, Sanders, the discipline hammered into them right here on this island. It's too late by the time they get to Korea."[12]

The Korean War ended in 1953, but the 1st Marine Division did not deploy from the former combat zone until 1955. In 1956 the recruit depots' younger DIs, the corporals and junior sergeants, were primarily those whose combat experience came during the static trench warfare, which began in 1951. It was the only combat experience they had, and they drew the wrong conclusion. Their experience indicated to them that the discipline taught in boot camp was the key to survival in a type of combat where a man functioned more as an individual than as part of a team. It quite naturally affected the way they trained their recruits. They were precisely the group of DIs who perpetuated the majority of the maltreatment incidents.

Surveys showed that the older NCOs—staff sergeants and above—were less likely to maltreat recruits. These more senior DIs were the ones most likely to have served in World War II or in Korea during its first year, before the breakdown of primary groups. The Marine Corps, however, interpreted these data as simply an indicator that older, more mature men were less likely to maltreat recruits.[13]

Two threads of the story now come together. First, Marines, and especially junior NCOs, believed that traditional forms of "discipline" provided the ultimate basis for the Corps' success in combat. Second, NCOs as a group used the autonomy of DIs for two purposes. It served the NCOs as a tool for teaching the importance of discipline to recruits as well as a means of shoring up their group's decreased authority and prestige. These two trends combined at Parris Island to create a pressure-cooker situation that fostered brutal treatment of recruits. In this atmosphere, the level of brutality reached unprecedented levels. Never before had recruits suffered so much. Senior Marine officers, unfortunately, lost touch with what was going on until Ribbon Creek blew the lid.

1

Development of the Maltreatment Problem

Formal recruit training for Marines began early in the second decade of the twentieth century; this task became Parris Island's primary mission in 1915.[1] Earlier recruits received their initiation into the Marine Corps as part of a "rookie squad" at their first duty station.

Typical of the training given rookies was the program at the Marine Barracks at Bremerton, Washington, in 1901. The routine began with thorough showers, after which the newly arrived men drew their uniforms from the quartermaster sergeant. The latter kept their civilian clothing; the recruits never saw them again. When the training began, the recruits did not even rate a corporal as their instructor; instead, a long-service private taught them the rudiments of close-order drill. Only then did they receive their Krag-Jorgensen rifles. Next, they learned such subjects as the manual of arms, bayonet fighting, and the loading, firing, and cleaning of the rifle. The final step in recruit indoctrination involved company-level tactics, including maneuvers directed by both voice and bugle calls.[2]

This simple training system suited a Marine Corps smaller than the police force of New York City.[3] It became increasingly impractical as the Corps grew in size, gradually assumed the new mission of capturing advanced bases for the Navy, and, at the same time, committed larger numbers of its ranks to expeditionary duty. The Corps needed a more formal arrangement for training and, in response, established small recruit depots under the auspices of other Marine organizations on both coasts. Such a training unit operated briefly at Parris Island in 1911 and reappeared there in 1915.

World War I brought on a great expansion at Parris Island. The instructors were experienced regular noncommissioned officers (NCOs) who, according to Marine author John W. Thomason, Jr., worked and drilled their recruits "from an hour before day until taps, and they never let up, and they never heard of mercy."[4]

The drill instructors of World War I apparently did not need to rely upon their fists to control their recruits. Thomason's fictional recruit once absentmindedly lit a cigarette in ranks after the instructor gave the platoon "at ease." According to the story, the sergeant, upon seeing the cigarette, grabbed the recruit's shirt and shook him violently while cursing him for his stupidity. Such a reaction from the sergeant obviously was quite unusual. The recruit, though well along in his training, was shocked. "Nobody had ever put his hands on me like that, or talked to me that way, in all my life."[5]

Don V. Paradis, one of the very few World War I veterans who fought in all the Marines' major battles in France without being wounded, also described his drill instructors as stern and demanding. They once punished Paradis by making him walk several miles carrying heavy buckets of sea water, but they never hit him or any other recruit. Even so, the hazing so affronted the personal dignity of Paradis and his fellow recruits that most refused to shake hands with the DIs upon completion of the training.[6]

In the two decades following World War I, during which the drill instructor became a Marine Corps institution, DIs continued, by and large, to refrain from using corporal punishment to discipline recruits.[7]

Brigadier General Samuel R. Shaw, who began his career as a "boot" at Parris Island in the 1920s, recalled:

> I went through Parris Island when it was supposed to be the old, tough Marine Corps. Nobody ever laid a hand on anybody in my platoon. We didn't have those things happen to us. Most of us were young men, and were being treated like men. We weren't no-account people who were slapped and kicked.[8]

Shaw related, however, that a footlocker improperly prepared for inspection might be tossed out the window. In addition, the platoon underwent considerable group punishment. For example, if one man swatted a "sand flea," one of the notorious biting gnats of the Carolina Low Country, everyone in the platoon did extra physical exercises. "But," recalled Shaw, "as far as anybody grabbing hold of any recruit and doing anything to him, or buckets over their head, or stuffing them into the foot lockers, or eating cigarette butts, absolutely not."[9]

Recruits of that era very well might not have submitted to such indignities. Retired Major Robert A. Smith, who underwent recruit training at Parris Island in 1929, recounted that his drill instructor's welcoming speech included a challenge. " 'I'm tough enough,' he said, 'to lick any man in this outfit; if anyone doubts it, step out!' So many recruits set out for him that he ordered them to halt. 'Okay, I only wanted to find out what I had to contend with.' " The DI then went on with his instructions as if the incident had not occurred. " 'From now on, wherever you go, you'll move on the double.' "[10]

First Lieutenant Wallace M. Greene, Jr., the officer in charge of drill instructors at San Diego in 1935, observed many years later that a similar willingness to protect themselves was expected of Marines. "No man," he wrote, "no Marine ever had to take a blow from another without the immediate right to retaliate—to protect himself—and to demand justice."[11]

Drill instructors had to be conscious of such attitudes among their charges. Further, the Marine Corps was so small that, in all likelihood, the former recruit would serve someday with his former drill instructor. Major Smith's recollections provide evidence of this. His drill instructor in 1929 made it clear that the drill instructor/recruit relationship was only temporary. "Until you men complete boot camp," said Smith's drill instructor, "you'll address me and all other DIs as 'Sir.' "[12]

The foregoing accounts provide one final important point: between the two world wars recruits were considered men, not boys. By and large they were men, either chronologically or in levels of maturity. During the lean years of the Great Depression, the Marine Corps could set its admission standards high. The superior quality of the enlistees of the depression years created something of an institutional memory of a "golden age." One Marine officer, writing two decades later about new approaches to training after Ribbon Creek, explicitly expressed this perception: "Alas for the days. . . . of the 30s and grateful adults sheltered from vagrancy by acceptance into a severely critical and selective military establishment."[13]

This halcyon era, with its high-quality recruits and frequent reenlistments, was one when even privates might have several years of service under their belts. As a result, privates who acted as drill instructors were not green, but experienced Marines. Officers gave DIs little supervision, yet these men could train a platoon of ex-civilians into Marines without the use of their fists or other corporal punishment. A common memory of the era was that of Colonel M. F. McLane, who wrote that "drill instructors—they were privates then . . . put my platoon through vigorous training [in 1934] without laying a hand on any of us."[14]

This does not mean that drill instructors did not punish their recruits; it means only that fists were not used. Retired Major R. A. Smith recalled instances of having to raise and lower his rifle over his head several hundred times, carrying buckets of sand for long periods, and pushing a wheelbarrow full of sand through other soft sand.[15]

Saying that drill instructors did not hit their trainees does not mean they did not induce their recruits to do so to recalcitrants in their midst. Major Smith's memoir specifically mentions the use of the belt line to punish recruits. He wrote:

> For the belt line, the platoon was formed in two ranks facing inward. Each man was issued a wide leather belt as part of his uniform. Grasping the buckle end of the belt, each man had to swing and hit the man being punished as he ran through. Whoever missed and was spotted by a DI also had to run through the line. Often, the DIs made us run through the line for no reason at all.[16]

A man who ran quickly would not be severely injured, especially since the DIs prohibited anyone hitting with the buckle end of the belt. However, Smith implied that on occasion a recruit might swing the wrong end. "Any man who used the buckle end on another going through the line," remembered Smith, "was made to run the course with all of us ordered to use our buckles on him. No one ever passed that test."[17]

Another familiar element of the Parris Island experience, the ubiquitous sand flea, continued to aid drill instructors in teaching discipline. Colonel Mitchell Paige, who enlisted in the 1930s and later earned the Medal of Honor and an officer's commission on Guadalcanal during World War II, vividly recalled such practices. While at the rifle range, Paige's instructor would march the platoon to a sandy area and then order them to stand at attention for an hour. In his memoir, *A Marine Named Mitch,* Paige recalled:

> With our arms and necks exposed since we could only wear an undershirt, the thousands of sand fleas were all over us, in our nostrils, eyes, ears, and hair. [The drill instructor, Corporal] Webb paced back and forth around us, pounding the palm of his hand with a stick and screaming, "If you move a muscle, I'll kill you!"[18]

The lesson taught by these sand fleas, though painful, was a valuable one, especially for Marines undergoing initial exposure to marksmanship at the rifle range. A man who could stand at attention while enduring such torment could also ignore distractions and concentrate on hitting the bull's-eye on the target. He would learn he was capable of ignoring the distractions of the battlefield and concentrate on hitting an enemy soldier with bullets from his weapon.

Mitchell Paige's drill instructor also believed in teaching march discipline. One night during the platoon's stay at the rifle range, Corporal Webb woke the platoon around 2:00 A.M. and ordered them to prepare heavy marching packs, carry these outside, and then put on the packs. Webb then marched the platoon into Ribbon Creek, while standing on the bank and yelling, "Drown, you dumb bastards, drown!" Paige remembered that his platoon was not that foolish; the front men marched straight across, the rest followed, and there were no problems or injuries.[19]

Corporal Webb and others did not hesitate to cause discomfort; nor did some drill instructors hesitate to fleece their recruits of money. Major Richard A. Smith experienced one of these rackets while a recruit. It occurred in the middle of the night. The DI suddenly turned on the lights and announced there would be a clothing inspection in fifteen minutes. All clothing not actually being worn by the owner had to be displayed on his bunk in a regulation manner. The recruits, still half asleep, had little time to lay out their uniforms properly. During the subsequent inspection, any item improperly displayed sailed out the window. Accomplices of the DI waited outside in the dark and picked up the articles and departed before the drill instructor finished inspecting. They found a ready market for clothing in those depression years either with civilians or with other Marines who wished to conserve their meager clothing allowance of $0.09 per day.[20]

Recruit training, despite its imperfections, became institutionalized during the late 1920s and the 1930s into much the same form as it existed in the 1950s and, to a certain extent, as it does today. With this institutionalization there developed a pride among Marines for the base where they underwent recruit training. Boot camp, whether at San Diego or Parris Island, attained the same reverence among enlisted Marines as could be found for an alma mater, fraternity, class, or athletic team among college graduates.[21]

World War II, with its great expansion of recruit training, strained the institution. Quite simply, the supply of qualified drill instructors never caught up with the demand. Often, only one of a platoon's team of DIs previously had taken a platoon through the training cycle. During the hectic first months of the rapid mobilization, many new assistant drill instructors worked with one platoon for only a short period before being given their own brand-new platoon to train. At least through the end of 1941, however, the drill instructors were experienced Marines, and not recent graduates of boot camp.[22]

The level of experience among the DIs began to change in 1942 as continued expansion eroded the absolute number and percentage of qualified, prewar Marines at Parris Island. Soon, as mentioned above, many of the DIs themselves had been recruits only a very short time previously. Since the instructors' qualifications varied, the nature and the methods of the training also varied from platoon to platoon. Bem Price, a twenty-seven-year-old newsman who enlisted for the Combat Correspondents Program, had "dedicated professionals" as his instructors in 1942. On the other hand, prominent newsman Jeremiah O'Leary, who later wrote of his recruit training at Parris Island, learned from instructors who were barely more experienced than their recruits.[23]

Punishments meted out by DIs also differed from platoon to platoon. Many veterans swear that their drill instructors never laid a hand on them. Others, like author William Manchester, remembered that "it was quite common to see a DI bloody a man's nose, and some recruits were gravely injured."[24]

Various forms of hazing and corporal punishment gradually crept into the system and eventually became common as the training load required the use of more and more recent recruit graduates as drill instructors. These young, inexperienced Marines had trouble asserting themselves with new recruits their own age. They relied upon their fists and heavy doses of profanity to gain ascendancy over recruits who could not hit back. The traditional practice of giving DIs great leeway and relatively little supervision, combined with supervision by officers and senior NCOs who themselves were relatively new to the Marine Corps, contributed to the increase in hazing and corporal punishment. Many drill instructors, too inexperienced to know enough to fill the hours with productive training, spent considerable time hazing their trainees.[25]

Some of the hazing would have been familiar to prewar Marines; other acts appeared for the first time. As in the past, DIs still marched their platoons in deep sand until people were ready to drop. Forcing recruits to stand at attention while ignoring sand fleas remained a standard practice. A new technique involved placing a bucket over an offender's head and making him smoke one or more cigarettes. The "field day," the Marines' term for a thorough cleaning of living spaces, changed from a necessary sanitary activity to a punishment invoked at odd hours.[26]

An earlier generation of recruits would not have stood for such treatment. The wartime ones did. Several factors contributed to their acquiescence. Patriotism, and the desire to fight for or at least serve one's country played a role. Additionally, the Great Depression tempered the wartime generation of Marines; they were used to hard times. Robert H. Barrow, who became Commandant of the Marine Corps many years after his wartime recruit training at Parris Island, stressed that the nature of the growing-up process in American society in those years meant that his platoon was about 90 percent "disciplined" before entering the Marine Corps. Jeremiah O'Leary said his Depression-reared generation knew how to survive and adapted quickly to the Parris Island regimen. Finally, as William Manchester recounted, they had the feeling that the war was something in which their entire generation was involved; even President Franklin D. Roosevelt's sons were in uniform.[27]

These factors helped keep maltreatment from becoming intolerable. In addition, the training system's orientation was toward pushing recruits through and out into the Fleet Marine Force. As a consequence, there was a gradual lessening of pressure on the trainees as they progressed through the training cycle. At a certain stage the barbers began trimming only the hair on the side of the recruits' heads. Another milestone was to be allowed to go to the post exchange. As recruits gained these little privileges and went through training events such as the bayonet course, each recruit could begin to feel "like a fighting man instead of a prisoner in a French penal colony."[28]

The size of the training establishment declined following World War II, but the hazing introduced during the war did not. Ralph Turtinan, who went through Parris Island in 1945 and later became a journalist, described a fellow recruit who had to "puff on a half-dozen cigarettes simultaneously with a bucket over his head." He also recalled recruits having to hold their rifles over their heads until they were ready to drop, and others receiving a swift kick in the rear end or a "tap" on the head from the DI's swagger stick for walking awkwardly.[29]

The Marine Corps made no significant effort to eliminate such practices. In fact, Marines in general believed the existing system met the Corps' needs well. The only question that arose was a minor internal one of just how the system worked to transform a civilian into a Marine. One Marine officer reportedly said, "Probably it's a good thing we don't know how it's done. If we knew, we might fiddlebitch and tinker with the process until we ruined it."[30] This statement overlooks the obvious pitfall: one cannot control a system one does not understand.

The Marine Corps did make minor changes in the program after the war. To ease the burden on drill instructors, the depot established special instructor sections to deliver classroom lectures on subjects ranging from personal hygiene and sanitation to scouting and patrolling. Previously, the drill instructors taught practically everything the recruits learned.

The base itself underwent a name change in 1947 from "Marine Barracks, Parris Island" to "Marine Corps Recruit Depot, Parris Island." The key elements of the drill instructors' role did not change; they remained the paramount instruments for teaching recruits such intangibles as pride, loyalty, discipline, and esprit de corps.[31]

The start of the Korean War in June 1950 brought turmoil to Parris Island again. The number of recruits increased 445 percent between June and September. This drastic expansion outran the supply of experienced drill instructors. To train new ones, the depot reestablished the drill instructors' school, which had been discontinued following the reorganization of the base in 1947. The new school, however, consisted essentially of a two-week briefing by veteran DIs.[32]

Other bases, following orders from Headquarters Marine Corps, had to transfer prospective DIs to Parris Island. The quality of these varied. Most commands tended to keep their best men and use Parris Island as a dumping ground for lower-quality NCOs. In one class at the DI school, almost 30 percent failed to complete the abbreviated course. Inevitably, as it had in World War II, the depot turned to the pool of recent recruit graduates to fill half its input of new drill instructors. The average age of these new DIs was nineteen years.[33]

The Korean War brought an increase in the amount of hazing and use of profanity. Recruits caught chewing gum marched with wads of gum stuck to their noses. Any recruit apprehended eating an unauthorized candy bar carried it in his hand for the rest of the day.

Those who lost their footlocker keys had to sew their spare keys to their caps, and thereafter open the box without removing the caps from their heads. Drill instructors also resorted to more severe punishments, ranging from jerking a recruit's cap down over his chin to a swift kick in the seat of the pants. Tom Bartlett, a *Leatherneck* magazine correspondent who went through Parris Island in 1952, wrote, "I remember being thumped on the gourd [i.e., being hit on the head], and for two days I had a size ten and a half double-E boot imprinted on the soft flab of my posterior."[34]

In addition to a higher incidence of such punishments, a change in training philosophy entered the system. In the past, drill instructors eased up on their trainees as they advanced through the program. During the Korean War, however, DIs came to believe in maintaining intense pressure upon their platoons throughout the training cycle. That cut both ways, for it also kept the DI under pressure for the duration of his tour on the drill field.[35]

Another development involved the perception of recruits. Prior to World War II, they had been looked upon as men. The literature of the early 1950s, however, almost invariably refers to them as "boys" and "children." Drill instructors were not the only ones using these terms. Admiral Thomas C. Kinkaid, USN (Ret.), used the phrase "undisciplined American boy" in a letter to a Marine officer after the Ribbon Creek incident. Brigadier General William B. McKean, in his book *Ribbon Creek,* described new recruits as "long-haired civilian children." Thinking of them as children permitted drill instructors to rationalize maltreatment: "We all spank our kids, don't we?"[36]

Most active-duty Marines everywhere held similar views about recruits and recruit training, as shown in a survey conducted in 1956. Despite evidence of a marked increase in the use of profanity to degrade an individual, a majority of Marines believed it had a valid use as a means of correcting a mistake or stressing a point. An aggregate of 79 percent believed hazing served the same purpose. These views were most noticeable in combat veterans, the group that dominated the ranks of drill instructors after Korea.[37]

The same survey documented the increase of profanity and hazing in recruit training. Of those undergoing boot camp prior to 1945, 23 percent said their DIs had used profanity "often," while 57 percent of the post-Korean War group gave the same response. Only 16 percent of the pre-1945 recruits encountered hazing on a frequent basis; the post-Korea group gave a 38 percent affirmative response.

Finally, the survey showed that abuses were noticeably higher at Parris Island than at San Diego.[38]

The Marine Corps knew of some of these trends early in the Korean War. By the fall of 1950 the inspector-general (IG) of the Marine Corps, Major General Samuel Howard, who had encountered maltreatment firsthand as a prisoner of war, had been receiving letters alleging incidents of mistreatment at Parris Island. He looked into this during his next scheduled inspection of the depot. His subsequent report to the Commandant included a supplemental report on "certain undesirable aspects of recruit training."

This report upset the G-3 Division at Headquarters Marine Corps. Since the G-3 had responsibility for overseeing all training within the Marine Corps, its officers resented the intrusion into their staff responsibilities, and requested from the Commandant that future IG inspections not cover recruit training. The Commandant agreed, and revised Marine Corps General Order 116 to contain this provision. Subsequent IG reports on Parris Island stated that the inspection had been solely an administrative one, and thus could make no conclusion on the ability of the depot to train recruits.[39]

Headquarters Marine Corps, including the Commandant, General Lemuel C. Shepherd, seem to have considered maltreatment at the recruit depots a problem, but not a major one. As a result, everyone appears to have taken reports of abuses as individual incidents rather than as part of an overall pattern.

One reason for this approach was the tendency of Marines to embellish their stories of the toughness of their own drill instructors. This tendency was especially apparent when the young Marine went home for the first time after completing boot camp. On occasion, such stories found their way into the hometown newspapers and generated angry letters to the Commandant and congressmen. Headquarters and the depots had a hard time separating the truth from exaggerations; inevitably, they took all such reports with a grain of salt.[40]

Headquarters Marine Corps did not let the matter drop entirely, however. Major General Merwin H. Silverthorn, who gave up his temporary rank of lieutenant general upon completion of his tour as the assistant commandant, took over Parris Island in March 1952. He arrived with specific instructions from the Commandant to eradicate maltreatment, a move possibly motivated by a picture story in *Life* magazine a few months before.

The *Life* article, published on October 8, 1951, chronicled the eight-week training cycle of a platoon commanded by "Parris Island's foremost DI," Staff Sergeant William S. Trope. The story, written with a favorable slant, passed quickly over minor acts of corporal punishment to concentrate on the heavy dose of hazing given new recruits.

None of the photographs showed a DI hitting a recruit, but one caption, found under a picture of a newly arrived recruit who was standing at attention improperly, noted that Sergeant Trope "came up, knocked his head forward, and pushed his stomach in." Some pictures showed the DIs jerking caps down over the faces of inept trainees as well as making one man hold a 9.5-pound M–1 rifle at arm's length for five minutes. Another recruit, who forgot to wear a belt, had to carry it in his mouth; another did the same with a shoe he neglected to put away. Further, Sergeant Trope used the one day of field training as a means of weeding out weaklings; at one point he twice marched the platoon past the prostrate form of an exhausted recruit. The article quoted Trope as saying, "I give them every chance to crack up." By graduation, however, the members of the platoon who remained said they understood the reasons behind Trope's methods and considered him the best kind of NCO to serve under in combat.[41]

In spite of this, the article depicted arts of hazing that many Americans would find demeaning. Worse, a perceptive reader would reach the conclusion that if these were the methods of the very best DI at Parris Island, the methods of the average DI might be very bad indeed.

Silverthorn's first order after his arrival at Parris Island laid down the law: drill instructors would not maltreat their recruits. The latter were to be treated as men, not boys. Many drill instructors resisted the order, and several received courts-martial for their disobedience.[42]

General Silverthorn put pressure not only on the DIs but also on their officers. He let the battalion commanders know unequivocally that he expected those who maltreated recruits would receive automatic courts-martial. Silverthorn reminded the officers that while regulations gave commanding officers some leeway on whether or not to prosecute, he did not. Those commanders who believed a case merited deviation from this policy had to visit Silverthorn and obtain his permission in each case.[43]

General Silverthorn made these instructions explicit in a memorandum to all battalion commanders, a memorandum that also revealed the pervasiveness of maltreatment problems at Parris Island. In it, Silverthorn directed that upon learning of a case of maltreatment, a battalion commander would confine the drill instructor and segregate all recruit witnesses. The memorandum continued: "It is well-known that many Drill Instructors have escaped punishment because they or their friends frightened the recruits into false testimony or in refusing to testify as to actual facts."[44]

General Silverthorn's efforts did not succeed, partly because the DIs became more secretive in their hazing and maltreatment, and also because the officers at the base would not support the general's policies. Officers overlooked minor acts of abuse toward recruits rather than elevate them to court-martial offenses. Battalion commanders tended to accept drill instructors' excuses and merely "chewed out" the man.[45]

Those cases that did come to trial usually did not result in convictions, especially in the lower-level special and summary courts-martial. Summary courts, the lowest form of military trials, and consisting of a single officer acting for both defense and prosecution, convicted only one DI in the three cases tried during Silverthorn's tenure at Parris Island. Special courts, normally composed at Parris Island of two officers and a DI from another battalion, had a similar record. Of the twenty-one DIs brought to trial before special courts-martial, only six were found guilty. Similar records of conviction rates occurred throughout the Korean War.[46]

General Silverthorn knew the reason behind the low conviction rates. Simply put, the courts were reluctant to convict a DI if the maltreatment did not disable the recruit or cause him to require medical treatment or hospitalization. In the latter cases, which went before the highest level of military court, called a general court-martial, the rate of conviction was high. During Silverthorn's period of command, there were twelve convictions out of the fifteen cases brought before general courts-martial.[47]

Marine officers in the male recruit training battalions at Parris Island obviously condoned acts of hazing and maltreatment that did not seriously injure recruits. Half of them, 50.8 percent, were veterans of the fighting in Korea; such men could be expected to believe in tough training. The majority of the officers, 68.62 percent, were reservists on active duty because of the war, and over one-third, 39 percent, had been on active duty for less than ninety days.[48] They were not a group that could be counted upon aggressively to eliminate tough training practices that increasingly strayed across the line into maltreatment. Silverthorn was stuck with them; his only alternative was to improve the selection and quality of DIs.

Continuing problems with the quality of potential drill instructors caused the Marine Corps to upgrade the drill instructors' school in October 1952. The new course lasted 3.5 weeks and had new admission requirements. Each student had to be at least twenty-one years old, have a General Classification Test (GCT) score of 100 or higher,[*] a neat appearance, self-confidence, the ability to deal with people, and a suitable voice.[49]

The Marine Corps modified these entrance standards in 1954, following the end of fighting in Korea. Whereas most students previously had been privates first class, the revised standards required the students to be NCOs, but lowered the minimum age to twenty and the GCT to ninety. Examinations by a psychiatrist became a regular part of the screening process.[50]

The revised standards meant that prospective drill instructors almost invariably would be veterans of Korea. It was precisely this group that the 1956 survey showed had the most favorable image of the effectiveness of boot camp. However, this group was not necessarily the best qualified to become drill instructors. The drill instructor school found that 60 percent of the prospective students did not meet its standards; of those accepted, only 60 percent completed the course. By extension, approximately 86 percent of the junior NCOs in the Marine Corps lacked the ability to train recruits.[51]

The introduction of the new admission standards, however, pleased Major General Silverthorn. He expected much from the NCO-level graduates of the school. Silverthorn expressed his pleasure at a graduation of new DIs in June 1954. In addition, by way of comparison, he said that many young drill instructors of the war years had lacked the maturity or age required to be effective on the drill field.[52]

---

[*] At this time, the Marine Corps tested new personnel with the Army General Classification Test. A GCT score equates roughly with an IQ Score. A score of 100 equals "average" or normal intelligence.

Drill instructors were not without their problems, which was to be expected given the pressure-cooker environment in which they worked. Their officers, their fellow instructors, and their own desire to excel pushed them toward the goal of producing good platoons.[53] Doing so taxed their leadership skills, since the indoctrination received at DI school told them what the regulations said they could *not* do, rather than what a DI could do to train recruits effectively.[54]

The stresses of the job gradually ground down the drill instructors. Among the stresses were the shortages in qualified drill instructors that were the norm for the mid-1950s. Each platoon was supposed to have three drill instructors; often there were less. To make up for this chronic problem, the DIs remained too long on the drill field. In the interim, they often moved from one graduating platoon to a brand-new one without any breaks. As one depot commander later admitted, these pressures on the DIs "sort of wore them out."[55]

In addition to these pressures, the new Uniform Code of Military Justice, introduced in 1950, and the Marine Corps' traditional system of minimal officer supervision of DIs worked together to reinforce the frequency and severity of maltreatment of recruits. The UCMJ, as originally written, restricted the legal authority to administer punishment to battalion and higher commanders.[*] Company commanders no longer could punish those guilty of minor offenses. However, the new legal system supposedly would eliminate those abuses of power by junior officers and NCOs that had so rankled the citizen-soldiers of World War II. Consequently, the new law required a drill instructor to take any offender before the battalion commander for punishment.

Drill instructors complained that the new legal system placed them in an untenable position. They claimed that if they took every offender before the battalion commander—a process involving filling out a charge sheet, scheduling office hours with the battalion commander, and bringing along witnesses—there would be no time left for training. Further, they said they feared that following such a procedure on a frequent basis would soon earn a DI the reputation of being a poor leader unable to control his troops. Finally, they expressed reluctance to report minor infractions that might earn a recruit a bad record and possibly an undesirable discharge.[56]

---

[*] A subsequent revision returned to company commanders the authority to administer nonjudicial punishment for minor offenses.

These protestations, however, were nothing more than a facade that provided rationalizations for the maltreatment of recruits. The UCMJ did provide NCOs with methods for correcting recruits or any other subordinate. It permitted "chewing out the recruit in a soft voice without profanity, obscenity, or abuse."[57] Additionally, the DI could conduct extra training of a constructive nature, which at Parris Island usually meant physical exercise. This included double-timing either in-place or around the parade field, push-ups, knee bends, duck walking, or using the rifle as a barbell. As General McKean noted, officers tended to give the "constructive nature" section of the rule a very broad interpretation, and ignored recruits involved in "chasing sea gulls" on the parade field or "staring at the Iwo Jima monument, ostensibly imbuing themselves with tradition."[58]

In those cases where extra physical exercises did not teach the inept recruit the proper lesson, the minimal officer supervision gave the DI the freedom to devise other but more surreptitious methods. Even though rarely disturbed by visits from officers, the DI could ensure absolute privacy by posting recruits to watch for officers. With this precaution, the only limit on the DI was his "ingenuity—and the avoidance of telltale marks. Even then a steady flow of minor injuries treated at Sick Bay [were] attributed with a straight face to flying locker boxes."[59]

There were a variety of punishments which would not leave marks upon the recruits' bodies. Among them were "elbows and toes," sometimes called "watching television," in which the recruit had to raise himself up on his elbows and toes while keeping his back straight. Another, suitable to Quonset huts whose inside roofs curved inward, involved the victim placing his toes, belt buckle, and nose against the in-curving walls. Both of these punishments quickly brought on excruciating pain as muscles strained to maintain the position.

The drill instructors could get away with using such methods because the training system traditionally involved little officer supervision. Thus, while the duties of the DIs were exceedingly onerous, those of the officers decidedly were not. Parris Island became, for officers, a quiet backwater, a peaceful interlude after years of hard service in two wars. They and their families enjoyed comfortable housing located near the river and shaded by enormous live oak trees festooned with Spanish moss. The base had an excellent golf course and the nearby tidal estuaries and Atlantic

Ocean offered superb fishing. Hunting in coastal Carolina was just as good. In addition, as one Marine general noted, the base was also a favorite of those officers addicted to heavy drinking and womanizing.[60]

The quiet backwaters of any institution do not attract the ambitious. Parris Island, in the years after the Korean War, became a favorite duty station for officers on their "twilight cruises" at the end of their careers. Younger, more ambitious officers tended to seek assignments elsewhere. When Major General Joseph C. Burger took over the base in January 1956, he found that, with some notable exceptions, his staff was merely average in professional quality. Further, while the depot rated only one warrant officer, there were as many as twelve assigned. Lieutenants were rare on Parris Island. Burger recognized the problem but had not made his final decision about a recommendation to the Commandant when the Ribbon Creek incident occurred.[61] An inertia, an inability or lack of desire to correct fundamental problems had crept into the training system.

Another indicator of the officer problem was that the little supervision the DIs did receive came primarily during normal working hours. At night the "officer of the day" supposedly kept an eye on what went on in the recruit training areas. It was not enough; even General Burger realized a lot of things went on at night at Parris Island that never came to light.[62]

The low level of officer supervision did more than permit abuses; it also affected the quality of Marines who became drill instructors at Parris Island. Little supervision resulted in little recognition for superior performance. "When you turn out a good platoon, they don't say anything," said Staff Sergeant Trope in *Life,* "and when you don't, they yell 'why?' "[63]

The depot, under these conditions, became equivalent to Siberia in the minds of many capable, ambitious Marine NCOs who were potential drill instructors. Too many of the best enlisted Marines, like the officers, sought assignments elsewhere. Parris Island made do with what it could get, and too many of these were misfits with chevrons.

Another noticeable characteristic at Parris Island in the years after the Korean War was a distinct hostility toward the young Americans enlisting in the Marine Corps. No more did one hear the recruits called men; "boys" is the universal term that appears in the accounts of the period. According to General McKean, a poll conducted some time before Ribbon Creek indicated that 80 percent of the DIs at Parris Island did not believe their recruits learned discipline at home when growing up. Most of them, 85.7 percent, believed the quality of enlistees had dropped since their own initial entry into the Corps. Many deemed corporal punishment a suitable tool in training the "boys" entering the Marine Corps. Even McKean, who commanded the Weapons Training Battalion prior to his retirement, believed a "moderate application" of corporal punishment would help salvage some of the "misfits" the depot discharged through its aptitude board. He also accepted that there would be a good bit of "laying on of hands" during the normal course of recruit training.[64]

Part of the hostility toward incoming recruits can be traced to a change in the motivations of enlistees subsequent to the Korean War. The Marine Corps falsely assumed, simply because the new recruits had signed enlistment papers, that it had received true volunteers. In actual fact, as Lieutenant General Robert H. Barrow admitted to Congress in 1976, the draft, rather than a desire for a military career, motivated many to enlist in the Marine Corps.[65] Military service was simply a fact of life to young men reaching maturity in the 1950s.

The Marine Corps, to most of them, was only a way station in their lives, rather than a potential home. Such young men had an entirely different motivation toward becoming Marines from their predecessors of only a few years before when enlisting meant combat service in Korea. The postwar enlistees were as much citizen-soldiers as the draftees serving in the U.S. Army. For the first time during a period of peace, the Marine Corps received a cross-section of the youth of America and attempted to train them using methods acceptable to the nation only in wartime. Middle-class America would not look favorably upon a system that mistreated its sons.

Included in the cross-section were black enlistees. Of all the services, the Marine Corps had been the most reluctant to accept full integration in the first place.[66] It had done so, but in 1956 there was not a single black drill instructor at Parris Island, presumably to avoid offending the community surrounding the base. Staff Sergeant Robert I. Edwards, the one black NCO who had managed to enter and complete drill instructors' school, worked at a menial job at the rifle range rather than as a drill instructor.[67] Blacks found a very ambivalent welcome at Parris Island.

Just as racial prejudice remained evident, so did the traditional schemes for cheating recruits out of their money. A DI could tell his platoon that his wife had to go to the hospital and he was short of cash (even though military dependents received free medical care). At Christmas some DIs would say that their families would not be getting many gifts because of a lack of money. Seldom would a "donation" not be forthcoming. When the command learned of specific cases, it found it difficult to prosecute the DI; neither the recruits nor other DIs would testify.[68]

Such refusals to testify took on additional significance as the rate of maltreatment spiraled upward, yet courts-martial continued to convict only the very worst offenders. Only nine of these came to trial in the fifteen months prior to the Ribbon Creek incident. The courts convicted only six. An example of those convicted was the case of a sergeant found guilty of hitting a recruit in the stomach nineteen times on his nineteenth birthday, kicking another in the stomach, beating a third with a swagger stick, and jumping on the stomach of a fourth recruit. During the trial, witnesses testified that the sergeant hoisted himself in the air by grabbing the tops of two bunks and then "mule-kicked" a recruit in the chest. The court acquitted the man of six other charges.[69]

Such cases were only the tip of the iceberg. When Brigadier General Wallace M. Greene, Jr., arrived at Parris Island in the aftermath of Ribbon Creek, he found ten recruits in the hospital with broken jaws.[70] He later described a similar incident in a letter to Colonel Robert D. Heinl, Jr. In his letter, Greene wrote:

> A drill instructor made a recruit *stand at attention while the instructor struck him repeatedly, breaking his jaw*. When the recruit fell to the deck, the drill instructor kicked him time after time. This was not an isolated incident, Bob—this was a common, everyday treatment which fortunately did not always put the recruit in the hospital.[71]

By January 1956, when Major General Joseph C. Burger took command at Parris Island, the level of corporal punishment and other abuses in the recruit training battalions had reached near explosive levels. Unfortunately, it was precisely at this point that the restraining pressure of command leadership lessened both on the Marine Corps in general and on Parris Island in particular. The new Commandant of the Marine Corps, General Randolph McCall Pate, who took office on January 1, 1956, was a more passive leader than his predecessors.[72] He did not immediately establish the firm grasp of command over the Marine Corps. As a consequence, Burger came to Parris Island with no sense of urgency; three months later he had yet to "dig in his spurs."[73] His light hand was insufficient for such a volatile situation. The element of "inevitable"[74] disaster awaited merely a time, a situation, and a place.

2

The Ribbon Creek Incident

Joseph C. Burger, then well into his second year as a major general, stood at the peak of an enviable career when he took command of the Marine Corps Recruit Depot, Parris Island, in January 1956. He had enjoyed an excellent professional reputation from the very beginning of his Marine Corps service when, as a second lieutenant, he played varsity football at Quantico. Later, as a captain, his company won the Breckinridge Trophy as the best unit among the Marines stationed in China in 1937. Burger performed equally well in combat in World War II, and had a good reputation among the upper echelons of the Marine Corps in the postwar years. Among these was Burger's friend and patron, General Randolph M. Pate, the new Commandant of the Marine Corps, under whom Burger served as assistant division commander of the 1st Marine Division in the closing days of the Korean War. In short, Joe Burger could reasonably count upon gaining his third star after a quiet tour at Parris Island.

General Burger arrived at Parris Island with no real sense of urgency about conditions in recruit training. Almost three months later, when the Ribbon Creek incident occurred, he still did not have a firm grasp on his command. Later many of his friends attempted to absolve him of blame for the incident because he had been in command for such a short time.[1] However, such apologies, though well meant, reflect little credit upon an officer who had reached high rank in a profession where "taking charge" was a cardinal virtue.

Burger was not entirely oblivious of conditions at the base, despite—if some of his critics are to be believed—a tendency for staff officers at the depot headquarters to filter the information reaching the new commanding general.[2] In the weeks before Ribbon Creek, Burger developed a vague perception of the maltreatment problem in the recruit training battalions. There were, he remembered later, one or two instances of recruits hospitalized with suspicious injuries, including one with a broken jaw. The injured man, however, insisted he had tripped over a footlocker while going to the toilet during the night and had hit his jaw against a nearby bunk. Burger recalled other recruits telling similar stories which may or may not have been true. He suspected these men were simply protecting their drill instructors. In any event, Burger said he could never quite put his finger on the problem.[3]

With no firm appreciation of the extent of the maltreatment of recruits, General Burger had no solutions to offer. Inevitably, he placed no pressure on his subordinates to control or eliminate recruit abuses.

On February 3, 1956, shortly after General Burger assumed command of the depot, Staff Sergeant Matthew C. McKeon graduated from the drill instructors' school. His class began with ninety students and graduated fifty-five. McKeon ranked fourteenth in the class, with a course average of 84.9 percent. This compared well with the 80.77 percent average set by students graduating in the previous two years.

Matthew McKeon, a thirty-two-year-old native of Massachusetts, was a lean veteran with more than ten years naval service who still retained a tendency toward occasional episodes of impulsive behavior. He served in the Navy in World War II on the aircraft carrier *Essex* from its initial commissioning until the ship's deactivation after the end of the war. He enlisted in the Marine Corps in 1948 and later served as a platoon sergeant of a machine gun platoon in the 1st Marine Division during the Korean War. Both McKeon and his wife were devout and active members of the Catholic church. They had two children and were expecting a third.[4]

Matthew McKeon had much for which to be thankful that February in 1956. His rank of staff sergeant placed him among the Corps' Staff NCOs, a position that carried considerable prestige among his contemporaries. Having become a drill instructor added to that prestige. These factors, plus service in two wars, assured him the chance for a full career as a Marine. His solid family life completed the happy picture. There was, however, one black spot in Matthew McKeon's life. He had considerable problems with a back injury, which, according to his later testimony, occasionally caused him considerable pain and increased irritability. This injury, however, did not hinder his progress through the strenuous drill instructors' school, which suggests it either was not on file in his medical records or doctors did not consider it serious enough to disqualify McKeon from attending the school. In any event, he later claimed his bad back played a role in his actions on April 8, 1956, and the injury ultimately provided the basis for his medical discharge from the Marine Corps in 1959.

Following graduation from the DI school, Staff Sergeant McKeon joined Company A of the 3d Recruit Training Battalion. The company commander, after giving McKeon further instruction on a DI's responsibilities, assigned him to be one of the three drill instructors of Platoon 71, which formed on February 23, 1956.[*] The most experienced member of this DI team, Staff Sergeant Edward A. Huff, served as the senior drill instructor. As such, he supervised McKeon and the other junior drill instructor, Sergeant Richard J. King.[5]

McKeon and King gained experience more rapidly than most new drill instructors by spending more hours than usual with their recruit platoon. They did not do so by choice. Staff Sergeant Huff, who was senior to McKeon, and who had sixteen months of service on the drill field, exercised his authority and assigned the two junior DIs to all-night and weekend duty. The platoon, as customary, received its swimming instruction at night, and Huff never took the platoon to the pool. When Platoon 71 moved to the rifle range, Huff rode out in his car; the two junior DIs marched with the platoon.[6] The officers of Company A either did not know of such practices or allowed them as the prerogatives of the senior DI.

Platoon 71 was not a very good recruit platoon by Parris Island's standards, and even its members recognized that fact. So did Staff Sergeant Huff, who, in his later testimony, said the platoon possessed less discipline than his previous four platoons. Several recruit members of Platoon 71 gave corroborating testimony.[7] Every military unit becomes a reflection of the qualities of its commander and, while inexperienced junior drill instructors may have been a contributing factor, Staff Sergeant Huff bears the primary respon-

---

[*] At that time, the two recruit depots numbered platoons serially as they formed. Later, they introduced a numbering system that prefaced each platoon number with the number of the battalion to which assigned. Thus Platoon 135 was the 35th platoon gained by the 1st Recruit Training Battalion in a given year. After Platoon 199, 1st Battalion's sequence would continue with Platoon 1001.

sibility for the platoon's poor quality and low morale. He simply does not appear to have provided the strong, decisive leadership necessary for creating a superior unit.

When the platoon moved to the rifle range for weapons training, it came under the overall supervision of the Weapons Training Battalion, commanded by Colonel William B. McKean. The colonel's chief claim to lasting fame as a Marine officer was his participation in a daring reconnaissance flight over the island of Guadalcanal in an Army B–17 a few weeks prior to the 1st Marine Division's August 7, 1942, landing on the island. The other Marine officer on the flight with Major McKean was Lieutenant Colonel Merrill B. Twining, a division operations officer. The aerial reconnaissance was only partially successful. Japanese float-planes attacked the bomber and drove it off before the two Marines completed their study of the proposed landing beaches.[8]

McKean had reached the pinnacle of his career by 1956. Even though only Major General Burger outranked him at Parris Island, McKean was not given the prestigious assignment of depot chief of staff, the number two job on the base. That position was held by Colonel Henry W. Buse, Jr., a highly regarded officer (he retired as a lieutenant general) who, at the time, was junior to McKean on the seniority list. This shunted McKean aside. Further, a selection board at Headquarters Marine Corps had passed over McKean when selecting officers for promotion to brigadier general. McKean, as a result, planned to retire on July 1, 1956, the first day of the new fiscal year. By leaving on that date, he would reap the benefit of any pay increases taking effect with the new fiscal year. Colonel McKean was under little pressure as he approached the end of his years as a Marine.

McKean could look forward to another plum upon his retirement from the Marine Corps. At that time the law permitted officers of the naval services who had been decorated for their combat performance in World War II to receive a promotion to the next higher grade upon retirement. Thus, for having received two Bronze Star medals, McKean would receive a "tombstone promotion" to brigadier general when he retired on July 1.[*]

---

[*] These tombstone promotions had prestige significance only; they carried no increase in retired pay. Congress abolished this provision in 1959; thereafter, regular officers of the naval services retired at the highest rank satisfactorily held.

April 8, 1956, was a typically quiet Sunday at Parris Island's rifle range, as well as for the rest of the base. Most supervisory personnel were elsewhere; only a few officers and NCOs had official duties to perform. General Burger, for example, was at the Masters Golf Tournament in Augusta, Georgia. Colonel McKean was at home. At the rifle range, the officer of the day and a few NCOs were alone in the headquarters offices. The sentries at the various posts were recruits, for guard duty formed part of their training. The bars at the various clubs were open for those Marines with no other place to go.

In Platoon 71, Staff Sergeant McKeon was the duty drill instructor for the weekend. His tour had begun at noon on Saturday. After he took the platoon to Sunday breakfast, the recruits went to either Protestant or Catholic church services. There was no training scheduled for Sundays. It could have been a quiet day for the platoon—except for the recurrence of McKeon's back problem. It caused severe pains in his leg and made him short-tempered.[9]

Around 10:30 A.M. Sergeant McKeon's touchy temper exploded when he observed several of his recruits using their smoking break outside Barracks 761 as an opportunity to lie on the grass. Such undisciplined behavior, in McKeon's view, could not be tolerated. He ordered the platoon to conduct a "field day," the Marines' name for the cleaning of living quarters that Army veterans remember as a "GI party." The recruits finished the job around 11:00 A.M., too short a time for a full-scale field day. Shortly thereafter, Technical Sergeant Elwyn B. Scarborough, the senior marksmanship coach assigned to Platoon 71 while at the rifle range, brought a half-full bottle of vodka into the room used by the platoon's drill instructors. For the next hour McKeon, Scarborough, and Sergeant Richard J. King drank from the bottle.[*] Around noon McKeon turned over his supervisory duties to King and went with Scarborough to the bar at the Staff NCO club. While the two men were at the club, King marched the platoon to the mess hall for lunch.[10]

McKeon returned to Barracks 761 with the platoon's mail between 1:30 and 2:00 P.M. King left the barracks sometime after McKeon returned; the latter then slept in his bunk for about an hour. Afterward he took the platoon to dinner at the mess hall between

---

[*] Sergeant King, as a bachelor, had to live in the drill instructors' room. There were no quarters set aside elsewhere on the base for bachelor DIs. This contributed to the maltreatment of recruits because bachelor DIs could not escape from the pressure-cooker environment of recruit training.

5:30 and 6:30 P.M. When they marched back to Barracks 761, McKeon released several recruits to attend either Protestant hymn-singing at the Old Depot Chapel or Catholic Novena at the new chapel. McKeon, still angry at the evidence of poor discipline in the platoon, and bedeviled by the sciatica in his leg, put the remaining recruits to work on still another field day in Platoon 71's barracks squadbay.[11]

Matthew McKeon was not an evil man. He wanted to be a good drill instructor and he strongly believed in the importance of military discipline. Platoon 71, however, did not seem to understand the necessity for discipline, and Matthew McKeon decided it was up to him to teach the lesson. A night march through the tidal marshes behind the targets of the rifle ranges, an area of ranges always called the "butts" by Marines, seemed the best way for demonstrating the value of discipline to Marines.

Several things probably influenced Sergeant McKeon's decision. First, as junior drill instructor, he had a strong desire to turn out a good platoon. Second, his painful leg had been bothering him all day. Third, he had consumed a number of drinks of vodka during the day; the bottle, still containing some vodka, remained in the room. At least one recruit saw McKeon drinking that evening. Finally, Parris Island folklore held that a night march in the tidal marshes was a good way to shape up a wayward platoon. These factors combined to produce a regrettable lapse in judgment.

By 7:30 P.M. Sergeant McKeon had made up his mind. He stuck his head through the doorway into the platoon's squadbay and announced, "You've got two minutes to fall out—we're going for a swim."[12] The platoon fell into ranks outside the barracks in the deepening darkness of a clear, moonless evening, and Sergeant McKeon marched them away. No one noticed them leave. The rifle range duty officer, who, by custom, toured the area only periodically, was at the rifle range theater supervising the showing of the evening movie.[13]

From Barracks 761, the platoon had to go across the main street through the rifle range area and then cross approximately 1,000 yards of open grass-covered ranges before reaching the edge of Ribbon Creek's marshlands. They arrived at the area between the butts of two of the ranges without being seen or heard, despite the fact that recruit sentries patrolled the entrances of the roads leading to the butts area of each range.

En route to the marshes, colloquially called "swamps" by Marines at Parris Island, Sergeant McKeon asked if there were any nonswimmers in the platoon. Several recruits answered, "Yes, Sir!" McKeon then jokingly remarked that all those who could not swim would drown; sharks would eat those who could swim.[14]

The platoon was approaching Ribbon Creek, a stream typical of coastal Carolina. The tidal estuary meanders through a marsh over 1,000 yards wide. One bend in the creek comes near the higher ground just behind Ranges C and D at Parris Island. The stream is over 200 feet wide at high tide, but narrows to about 100 feet at low tide. The banks and bottom are covered with a dark, viscous mud that slows movement. Marsh grass grows everywhere except in the channel where the water gets too deep. At low tide, the water in Ribbon Creek was generally shallow—about three feet deep—in the channel. Unfortunately for Platoon 71, the tide was high.

Matthew McKeon had not taken the tide into consideration. At 7:30 P.M. that Sunday night, the tide was still high but ebbing. The official high tide occurred at 6:34 P.M. However, experienced local watermen knew there was about a forty-five minute delay between high tide at the official measuring station and Ribbon Creek. Thus, when the platoon entered the water, Ribbon Creek was still near its maximum depth, but the outgoing current was picking up speed.[15]

The high tide was not the only problem. Out of ignorance of the area, McKeon was leading the platoon into the part of Ribbon Creek that contained what local fishermen called a "trout hole," a deeper area in the bend of the stream behind the butts area. The trout hole was over 100 yards long and averaged at least six feet in depth even at low tide.[16]

When they reached the marshy edges of the area behind Ranges C and D, Sergeant McKeon led the platoon into the water out to the point where it was from knee- to waist-deep, depending upon the individual's height and the extent to which those ahead of him had churned up the mud. This was near the edge of the trout hole. Sergeant McKeon, however, turned right and continued parallel to the curving bank for about thirty yards.* He then led the column in a left turn so that it moved parallel to its original path, but in the

---

* Had he led the platoon straight ahead, he would have led them directly into the trout hole. If so, he would have known the danger, and probably halted the platoon before most of his men even entered the water. Unfortunately, he chose to keep them in what he assumed was shallow water near the banks of Ribbon Creek.

opposite direction. This turn also took the platoon into somewhat deeper water. The water was now waist to shoulder deep, again depending upon the individual's height and place in the column. Further, the platoon was approaching the edge of the drop-off into the trout hole.[17]

On at least two occasions, Staff Sergeant McKeon asked if everyone was okay. Each time, after receiving affirmative answers, he moved into slightly deeper water. At least once he advised the recruits to stay in the shadows when moving in a stream at night in combat.[18] He also hit a recruit on the leg underwater and yelled, ''Shark!''[19]

Now, after at least fifteen minutes in the water and mud, the platoon's luck ran out. The outgoing tide nudged some recruits into the deeper waters of the trout hole. Several suddenly found themselves in water over their heads. The nonswimmers among them panicked. They desperately tried to keep their heads above water. The dark night filled with their screams for help as they grabbed for anything or anyone that might save them. The panic spread, perhaps fueled by the fears raised by McKeon's earlier cry of ''shark.'' McKeon himself did not panic. He shouted for everyone to get out of the water.[20]

Matthew McKeon had the courage and coolness to act in an emergency. He immediately swam out to the recruits who were shouting for help. He helped first one man to shore and then another. A terrified third recruit, however, grabbed McKeon, and they both went under water. McKeon managed to get himself and the man back to the surface where he tried to calm the panic-stricken recruit. It did not work, and they went under again. While under water the second time, the man let go of McKeon, who never saw him alive again. Meanwhile, Private Thomas C. Hardeman, one of the best swimmers in Platoon 71, also went to the aid of those calling for help. He did not return.[21]

Private Lewis Brewer saw Private Norman Wood in trouble and swam to him. Wood, in his panic, grabbed Brown, and both went under. When Brewer finally reached the surface, he could not find Wood. ''We were all mixed up,'' recalled Private Francis Armitage, ''guys were screaming, grabbing on to each other.''[22]

According to seventeen-year-old Private Thomas Grabowski, some clearheaded recruits organized a human chain to assist their fellows out of the water. Such actions saved lives; soon all the survivors were on shore. Staff Sergeant McKeon was the last man to leave the dark, now quiet waters of Ribbon Creek.[23]

Word of something unusual going on near Ribbon Creek already had begun to stir the rifle-range command system. A recruit sentry heard the commotion down near the creek and telephoned the sergeant of the guard. The latter went to investigate and found the cold, wet members of Platoon 71 on the banks of Ribbon Creek. The sergeant of the guard quickly notified the Weapons Training Battalion duty officer, Captain Charles Patrick, who, in turn, telephoned Colonel McKean.

The colonel was in his quarters watching the "Ed Sullivan Show" on television. His wife had fallen asleep during the program. The ringing telephone ended the McKeans' peaceful evening. McKean picked up the telephone and identified himself.

> "Colonel, this is Patrick. We're in trouble."
> "What's the scoop, Pat?"
> "Some knucklehead DI took his platoon to the swamp. They're streaming back to Building 761, cold, wet, muddy. Some [are] still lost."
> "What platoon and battalion?"
> "Don't know yet. [Sergeant] Taylor discovered them and reported it to me. I'm on my way to investigate."
> "Call me when you find out. Lock up the DI. Send those that need it to Sick Bay."[24]

Captain Patrick went to Platoon 71's squadbay and identified the platoon and its battalion. A muster revealed eight men missing. Captain Patrick telephoned Colonel McKean again. The latter said he would notify the depot chief of staff, Colonel Buse. He also told Captain Patrick to call him if there were anything new.[25]

Colonel McKean hung up the telephone and then decided not to wait for another call. He drove out to the C-Range butts where the search for the missing had already begun. The rescue workers found one live recruit on the other side of Ribbon Creek. Captain Patrick, who was at the site also, reported that a second missing recruit had been in sick bay and missed the march. There were still six men unaccounted for.[26] There would have to be a thorough, systematic search for them.

Word of the night march had reached General Burger by this time. He had returned from Augusta late that Sunday afternoon and, tired from the trip, had gone to bed early. Colonel Buse awakened him with a telephone call to report the incident and the missing six men.

Buse told General Burger that no one knew if they had drowned, and it probably would be morning before they knew for sure.[27]

These official notifications were not the only way information on the incident spread. The Marine grapevine passed the word in nearby Beaufort, South Carolina, where many of the married men lived. Marines informed their friends, "There's trouble at Weapons. I can't tell you what it's all about. You'd better get back to the Battalion." These Marines filtered in for the rest of the night, ready to help in the emergency.[28]

Marines were not the only ones in Beaufort who got wind of an incident at Parris Island. A stringer for the Associated Press (AP) also learned that something had happened at the Marine base. He notified the AP regional office in Charlotte, North Carolina, which, in turn, put out an advisory message over its teletype wires to AP's subscribing newspapers. The advisory said an official announcement could be expected shortly. Editors all over the country received this advisory in the midst of making up their Monday-morning editions. If the story proved important, they would have to make changes in their layouts. They waited.[29]

At Parris Island the Marines first assumed the missing men were alive and somewhere in the marshes. Recruits, on occasion, had tried to escape Parris Island, only to be found later in the salt marshes. Not until after midnight did the possibility of drowning enter Colonel McKean's head. Not until sometime Monday did he give up hope that some of the missing men might be found alive.[30]

General Burger and Colonel Buse came out to the banks of Ribbon Creek shortly after daylight on Monday, April 9, to check on the progress of the rescue efforts. They talked with Colonel McKean and discussed, among other things, notifying the newspapers. They faced a dilemma. If the missing men were still alive, it would be best, they agreed, to keep quiet. They did not want unfavorable publicity. If the men were dead, however, any delay would make the depot's position untenable. They also talked about the man who led the march. Staff Sergeant McKeon was already in confinement, and General Burger believed it best he remain there for his own protection. Burger was concerned that the despondent Marine might take his own life if not confined. After talking a while, the three officers decided to wait a little longer before making any announcement. However, as Burger and Buse departed, the latter told McKean that if the missing men were not found by 7:45 A.M., Burger would have to telephone General Randolph M. Pate, the Commandant of the Marine Corps.[31]

The men would not be found by the deadline. In fact, not until Thursday of that week would Marines pull the body of the last victim, Private Hardeman, from the deep waters of the trout hole.[32]

The nation's morning newspapers hit the streets as usual that Monday, but they carried no mention of a tragedy at Parris Island. Their editors' publication deadlines had passed without the news release predicted by the AP advisory. This had a major impact on the way editors approached the story later. What began as editorial impatience for further information changed to a growing suspicion that the Marines had something to hide. As the delay lengthened well into Monday, the curiosity and professional interest of newsmen grew. They began to anticipate a major story. They had to wait, however, until seventeen hours after the recruits died. When the Marine Corps finally put out its initial press release that Monday afternoon, it had the full attention of the entire national news media.[33]

3

The Immediate Reaction

Headquarters U.S. Marine Corps occupied the southwest end of the Navy Annex, a tan brick, comb-shaped, multistoried building situated on a ridge overlooking the Pentagon in Washington, D.C. Many members of the Headquarters staff were already at work when Major General Burger's telephone call came through from Parris Island early Monday morning, April 9, 1956. Most senior officers were at their desks. However, General Randolph McCall Pate, the new Commandant of the Marine Corps, was visiting his alma mater, the Virginia Military Institute, in Lexington, Virginia, to give a speech.[1]

When his staff reached him in Lexington, Pate immediately decided he had to go to Parris Island. He gave orders for the inspector-general of the Marine Corps, Brigadier General Carson A. Roberts, to join him there. Pate later said he went to Parris Island to see that depot officers properly handled the incident and to ensure that such a thing could never happen again.[2] However, the effect of his direct involvement was to draw even greater media attention to the tragedy.

Such abrupt decisions and actions were typical of Pate's performance while Commandant and made him probably the most controversial holder of that office in the twentieth century. General Pate was more attuned to the quiet pre-World War II garrison years than the hectic Cold War of the 1950s. He was more interested in appearances than substance. As Commandant he spent as little time as possible in Washington, preferring instead the honors and deference Marine commands gave a visiting Commandant. His erratic behavior and judgment caused many of his closest associates to worry about the state of his physical and mental health.[3]

Probable illness aside, there were other reasons Pate was not popular as Commandant. Retired Brigadier General Samuel R.

Shaw described Pate as an intelligent officer with fine ideas but few firm convictions about what the Marine Corps was or should be. His convictions always had been those of his boss, a trait that helped to further his career as a staff officer. However, as Commandant, a position requiring strong convictions based upon much previous thinking, Pate was beyond his depth.[4] As a result, he was far more passive and a creature of his staff than his predecessors had been.[5]

With Pate en route to Parris Island, the Headquarters chief of staff, Lieutenant General Vernon E. Megee, began orchestrating the action of the staff. One of the first he called in was Colonel James D. Hittle, who for the past three years had been the legislative assistant on the staff and who had close contacts on Capitol Hill. Megee's summons was one of the Corps' key moves in the management of the Ribbon Creek crisis.

Hittle was in his office in the second wing of the Navy Annex when the buzzer rang on his intercom.

"Please come down to my office," said Megee.[6]

When Hittle arrived, General Megee minced no words. He said there had been a tragedy at Parris Island in which some Marines had been drowned due to a drill instructor's mistake.

"There's going to be a press conference down at Parris Island very soon announcing it, and I want to let you know about it."

This sent a cold chill down Hittle's back, for it was his responsibility as legislative assistant to keep key members of Congress informed of Marine Corps affairs. His experience on Capitol Hill convinced him that the announcement, regardless of how bad it might be, should not be made without first alerting the Corps' allies in Congress.

"I have just one request," replied Hittle. "How long before that press conference?"

"Well," answered Megee, "very soon now. I've been told by telephone."

"Well, if there is any way of doing it," pleaded Hittle, "call them back and tell them to hold it at least an hour if they can, even if they have to bar the door."

Colonel Hittle left the chief of staff's office and immediately jumped into a car and went directly to Capitol Hill. Within the next hour, he saw and alerted Representatives Carl Vinson and Dewey Short, plus Senators Leverett Saltonstall and Richard B. Russell, all of whom were very strong supporters of the Marine Corps and who held key leadership positions in the House and Senate Armed

Forces committees. Their support was especially vital to the Marine Corps that April because both Armed services committees were in the midst of their annual hearings on the defense budget. The Marine Corps was counting on its friends in Congress to ensure that the Corps received its fair share of the austere defense appropriations requested by the Eisenhower administration.

Hittle went to Capitol Hill with two immediate objectives, one of which was to exercise the courtesy of keeping these powerful legislators informed. In addition, neither he nor Megee wanted any of these legislators to make a public statement without knowing the seriousness and incompleteness of the available information, especially since such a statement might commit them to some kind of action that they and the Marine Corps would later regret.[7]

Hittle's efforts succeeded. Following the official announcement of the deaths at Parris Island, none of the men Hittle contacted made statements that contained any commitment other than the intention of waiting for further word that would clarify the situation at the recruit depot.

While Hittle briefed the Corps' friends on Capitol Hill, an officer in the Headquarters Marine Corps public affairs section telephoned Parris Island's own public affairs officer, Captain Ralph C. Wood. The latter learned that not only was he to delay notifying the press, but also that the Washington office would draft the approved release. Wood did not like the idea; he liked it even less when a Headquarters staff officer called back and dictated a short news release over the telephone. The news release said:

> Six Marines are missing from the Marine Recruit Depot at Parris Island, South Carolina following a night training exercise conducted last evening.[8]

This short paragraph was a public relations disaster. On a purely humanitarian level, the failure to give a platoon number needlessly frightened thousands of families with sons in training at Parris Island.

On a professional level, the contents of the release put the Marine Corps under a cloud that persisted for months in the minds of newsmen. First, the release misled the press, however unintentionally. To a generation of editors and reporters that had matured during World War II and Korea, the use of the word "Marines" suggested a far greater level of experience and military competence than the more accurate word "recruits." The latter word should have been used, given the depot's well-known reputation for recruit training. Second, the phrase "night training exercise" implied the event was an unfortunate accident that occurred during a normal, scheduled part of training. It did not take an exceptionally astute editor to wonder why a routine training accident would require such a long delay in making an announcement. Finally, the news release contained so little information that no editor could publish the story without much more detail.

Captain Wood anticipated further press queries and made careful arrangements for handling them. All information on the progress of the rescue efforts would come to his office. He, in turn, planned to answer all questions from the press and give no official reply until he had all the facts.[9]

Captain Wood's office gave the news release to the United Press and the Associated Press at 1:00 P.M. on April 9, 1956. The International News Service (INS) received the story a few minutes later.[10] Within minutes, every editor in the country had the release. Radio stations had the story in plenty of time for their 1:30 P.M. news programs, and thousands of recruits' parents, upon hearing the sketchy news, became fearful for their sons' safety. At about the same time, editors were telling reporters to get busy on the story. The results were inevitable: hundreds of people all over the United States simultaneously reached for their telephones and called Parris Island.

Incoming telephone calls from the press quickly became so numerous that Captain Wood's plan unraveled within an hour. It proved almost impossible to get the latest information out to the press. Calls from worried parents added to the confusion in the public affairs office. To handle the load of calls, the telephone company in nearby Beaufort hurriedly began bringing in extra telephone operators. The surge of incoming calls, most of which were from worried parents, did not slacken for almost twenty-four hours, simply because the initial news release did not give the platoon number.[11]

General Pate arrived at Parris Island around 4:30 P.M. and immediately met with Major General Burger. They discussed the drowning incident in detail. By this time Burger had a good idea of what had happened at Ribbon Creek and gave Pate a thorough briefing. Then the two officers, accompanied by Brigadier General Roberts, visited the site of the tragedy, where Colonel McKean headed the search for the missing bodies. The recovery team had found the first body around noon and the fifth shortly before the group of generals arrived.

Pate, seeing the recovery efforts well in hand, turned to the cause of the incident. He asked Colonel McKean if the Weapons Training Battalion or the depot had any published order that forbade night marches in the tidal marshes. McKean replied that he recalled no order that would apply. Pate insisted: "There has to be something to cover this." McKean reiterated that, to the best of his knowledge, no such regulation existed.[12]

The three generals returned to Burger's office where they quickly recognized that a press conference was unavoidable. Newsmen, unable to get additional information over the jammed telephone system, had begun arriving at the base shortly after Pate. This was the start of a procession of arrivals that would last most of the night.[13]

General Burger, realizing the importance of the impending press conference, cautioned Pate that the newsmen would like him to make a lot of accusations. Burger advised Pate to say little other than that he did not wish to discuss details of the case until the court of inquiry, scheduled to convene the next day, completed its investigation. Pate agreed, and the two Marines drafted a statement conforming to Burger's recommendations. It also said Pate would personally review whatever action Burger took on the findings of the court of inquiry.

As he accompanied Pate to the meeting with the waiting newsmen, Burger was confident the conference would come off well. His confidence was misplaced, for, to Burger's dismay, Pate deviated from the agreed-upon plan. After reading his prepared statement, Pate unwisely agreed to answer questions. One reporter quickly asked if Sergeant McKeon were not guilty of breaking regulations. Pate replied, "It would appear so." The answer completed Burger's discouragement. He realized Pate had for all practical purposes accused McKeon of manslaughter before the court of inquiry even convened.[14]

There were a number of other questions from the assembled reporters. These ranged from McKeon's marital status to whether or not he had the authority to "discipline" his men. Other newsmen asked about formal arrangements for the funerals of the dead recruits. Pate's answers were short, but not evasive. He concluded the interview with the statement that the press was free to interview

any person on the base, including Staff Sergeant McKeon. "We
have nothing to cover up," he asserted.[15]

While Pate visited Parris Island, officers back at Headquarters
Marine Corps fervently discussed how the Corps should handle the
whole affair. One group, which included Major General David M.
Shoup, advised, "Do nothing. It will go away. Actions like this are
bad, but they can happen." Shoup and others wanted Burger to hold
a routine investigation, while Headquarters Marine Corps would
make no more statements until its completion.[16]

A group of more junior officers, which included Colonels Samuel
R. Shaw, Ormond R. Simpson (Pate's military secretary), James C.
Murray, and Hittle, believed a more carefully crafted handling of the
case was mandatory. They saw the incident as a national-level
problem for the Marine Corps that would bring congressional and
press scrutiny as well as provide ammunition for the Corps' enemies. In their view, there had been too many accusations of brutality
at Parris Island for Ribbon Creek to just fade away. They argued
that treating it in a "routine" manner would not work. They stressed
the need for a plan that would provide the Marine Corps with an
"out" and keep it from being "slashed."[17]

When Pate returned from Parris Island, Shaw and Simpson went
into his office to discuss the matter with him. They explained the
political dangers in detail.

"I understand; that's right," agreed Pate. "Now, what do you
recommend that we do?"

The two colonels replied, "We recommend that you get hold of
General Twining and bring him back here and have him be the
quarterback of whatever action we decide to [take]. We simply
know that we have enormous trouble. We don't have a good out for
it and we need an out that works, and the one to do it will be
Twining. [We] young sprouts . . . can't carry the day against those
generals who think that nothing ought to be done."[18]

General Pate made one of the best decisions of his tenure as
Commandant. He reached out, picked up his telephone, and placed
a long-distance call to Major General Merrill B. Twining at Camp
Pendleton, California.

Major General Twining, a fifty-three-year-old Naval Academy
graduate, had a well-known reputation for his dedication to the
Marine Corps and for his brilliance as a tactical planner in the Pacific
during World War II. As a colonel at the Marine base at Quantico,
Virginia, after the war, he was a key member of the Special Board

that developed the concepts that matured into the Corps' helicopter doctrine of "vertical envelopment." Twining also commanded the 1st Marine Division in Korea following the armistice that ended the fighting there. Now he had command of that same division at its peacetime home at Camp Pendleton. Many Marines considered Twining to be Pate's likely successor as Commandant.[19]

Pate's telephone call reached Twining at his quarters at about 5:00 A.M., California time. Pate gave him a brief outline of the Ribbon Creek problem and said he wanted Twining to come to Washington and personally manage the crisis for the Marine Corps. Pate added that he was having reservations made for Twining on a 9:00 A.M. flight from Los Angeles to Washington.[20]

General Twining had hardly hung up his telephone before another call came in from Washington. It was Simpson and Shaw. As soon as they had left Pate's office, they telephoned to give Twining all the information they had so that he could begin making plans during his flight east.[21]

General Twining made a hurried departure from Camp Pendleton. A Marine helicopter flew him from the base to Los Angeles to catch his plane to Washington.[22]

Twining arrived in the capital late that day, April 12, 1956. That evening he had dinner with Pate at the Commandant's quarters at Washington's Marine Barracks. The two officers discussed the Ribbon Creek situation. Pate said he wanted Twining to act as his ad hoc chief of staff in devising the Corps' response to the Ribbon Creek incident. Pate added that Lieutenant General Megee was too involved in writing a speech to superintend the effort. The Commandant also informed Twining that, unless the latter persuaded him otherwise, he intended to relieve General Burger of his command at Parris Island.[23]

The following morning, Twining set up shop in Colonel Hittle's office, which was next to Shaw's. One of the first things in the office that Twining noticed was a mess table stacked with hundreds of manila file folders. He looked through the folders and was shocked to find they contained thousands of earlier letters from congressmen concerning constituents' complaints about recruit training abuses. He read only a few. One of these, a letter he would always remember, described how a recruit had been required to stand on a table and repeatedly proclaim, "My mother is a whore!" All of the

This aerial photograph shows Parris Island's rifle range and the view looking toward "Mainside." Staff Sergeant Matthew McKeon led his platoon from one of the barracks in the center of the picture, across the ranges to the left, and into Ribbon Creek (out of the photograph). *Parris Island Museum*

General Randolph McCall Pate became Commandant of the Marine Corps only a few months before the Ribbon Creek tragedy at Parris Island, South Carolina in April 1956 which became the first major controversial issue of his tenure in that office. *Dept. of Defense Photo (USMC) A402599*

Brigadier General Wallace M. Greene, Jr., received sudden orders to Parris Island to conduct the formal pretrial investigation of the drowning of six recruits in the tidal stream known as Ribbon Creek. *Dept. of Defense Photo (USMC) A407502*

Major General David M. Shoup (right), the burly recipient of the Medal of Honor for valor on Tarawa in World War II and also the Marine Corps' newly-appointed Inspector General for Recruit Training, inspects an honor guard at Parris Island in May 1956 accompanied by Brigadier General Wallace M. Greene, Jr. *Historical Files, Marine Corps Historical Center, Washington, D.C.*

Brigadier General Wallace M. Greene, Jr., the man sent to Parris Island to institute reforms in Marine recruit training, removes his rank insignia before a man-to-man talk with the members of the ill-fated Platoon 71, the survivors of the Ribbon Creek tragedy, on their graduation day from "boot camp." *Historical Files, Marine Corps Historical Center, Washington, D.C.*

Attorney Emile Zola Berman and Staff Sergeant Matthew C. McKeon confer during a break in the latter's court-martial at Parris Island in 1956 for the deaths of six recruits who drowned in Ribbon Creek. *Robert Kelley,* Life *Magazine © Time, Inc.*

This sweltering, unairconditioned school building on Parris Island served as the site of the court-martial of Staff Sergeant Matthew McKeon in the summer of 1956. *Parris Island Museum*

Recruits at Parris Island practice bayonet fighting sometime in the early 1960s with the same aggressiveness that the Marine Corps traditionally has sought to develop in its Marines. *Parris Island Museum*

thousands of letters, Twining noticed, had something in common: each had been answered with a form letter from Headquarters Marine Corps.[24]

Those thousands of letters implied a great danger to the Marine Corps. They represented a ticking bomb that could explode if disturbed by a congressional investigation. Congress had been quietly complaining for years about training abuses, and the Marine Corps had taken no significant action to correct the problem. Any investigation that brought the whole situation accurately into public view—combined with the Corps' poor track record in this area——could easily push Congress into deciding to exercise its legislative powers to end abuses. The Marine Corps had to take decisive action to put its own house in order or face the strong possibility that Congress itself would take on the job.

Twining got busy. He called in a group of Marine officers experienced in Washington politics and in whom he had confidence. They began hammering out a plan and, by that afternoon, had decided upon the general format for the Corps' efforts.[25]

The first steps in the plan already had been taken by Don Hittle while Twining was en route from California. Hittle had visited Representative Carl Vinson, who agreed to issue a press release saying the House Armed Services Committee, of which Vinson was the chairman, would receive a full report from the Marine Corps the following week. The release added that the committee would then decide whether to hold a full investigation.

This gave the Marine Corps time to prepare its case. In addition, because of the protocol between the House of Representatives and the Senate, once the Armed Services Committee of either chamber announced plans for hearings on a matter, the other committee would not schedule duplicate hearings. Thus Vinson's statement also prevented action by the Senate Armed Services Committee. This meant the Marine Corps would be able to state its case before the friendly House Committee chaired by Vinson, whose long support for a strong Navy and Marine Corps had earned him the nickname of "Mr. Navy" in Washington.[26]

Vinson also realized the advantage of retaining the political initiative. He let the Marine Corps know through Hittle that he had decided to hold a hearing at which he expected the Commandant personally to appear and make his report to the House Armed Services Committee. This example of congressional action would probably satisfy the journalists from radio, television, and newspapers, as well as others who might be standing in the wings to criticize the Marines for any number of reasons. Vinson wanted to protect the Marine Corps, not see it torn apart in the press or in the Congress.[27]

Vinson was not the only legislator contacted by the Marine Corps, nor was Hittle the only Marine officer who visited Capitol Hill. Twining sent several officers, including Hittle, Colonel DeWolf Schatzel, Colonel Robert D. Heinl, Jr., and others to visit numerous congressmen and find out what Marine Corps action would satisfy them. These officers coordinated their efforts with John R. Blandford, one of Vinson's senior staff assistants who, providentially, happened to be a lieutenant colonel in the Marine Corps Reserve.

No one neglected the Senate's sensibilities either. Hittle, for example, met frequently with William Darden, a senior staff member of the Senate Armed Services Committee. Hittle also visited and briefed Senators Saltonstall and Long of that committee.[28] In return, these personal contacts provided Twining and his team with invaluable insights into the attitudes and expectations of Congress regarding the Ribbon Creek affair.

Carl Vinson passed information to Twining that he expected genuine action, not a coverup, from the Marine Corps. He said:

> "If your Commandant comes up here and tells me that he knows of no problems down there [at Parris Island], I will refresh his memory. I have in my possession at least 200 complaints which I have brought to the attention of your headquarters over the past few years which I will be glad to bring to his personal attention."[29]

These exchanges of information with Congress were crucial to the Marine Corps in formulating its plan for preventing the Ribbon Creek affair from becoming a full-blown national issue. Twining's team believed that it would be far better for the Marine Corps to put its own house in order rather than pass the initiative to Congress. The team believed that 1956 was doubly dangerous because it was an election year. If Ribbon Creek became an issue in the congressional election campaign, the Marine Corps system of training could be jeopardized. The team moved aggressively to placate the leadership of both the House and the Senate. These powerful leaders could help control junior congressmen and senators who, facing a tough election campaign and aware of public indignation over the Ribbon Creek incident, could have turned it into a hot campaign issue. Any incumbent with an inkling of the extent of maltreatment at Parris Island could make public revelations and call for a full congressional investigation. If a single incumbent raised the issue in his campaign, the others might be forced to do likewise or find their opponents using it against them. It was therefore in the Marine Corps' best interests to get the whole affair settled quickly, well before the campaign season.[30]

General Twining, in the midst of this activity, also had to draft the statement the Commandant would read in his testimony before the House Armed Services Committee. The statement had to be good if it were to defuse the Corps' opponents and save the recruit training system. It also had to restore the confidence of the American public in the Marines' training methods.[31]

The draft statement embodied all the elements of Merrill Twining's plan. The key element was straightforwardness. Pate and the Marine Corps would accept full blame and admit there were structural problems in the recruit training establishment. The Commandant would order an immediate restructuring of the system, including the establishment of new Recruit Training Commands at the two recruit depots. A brigadier general would head each of the new commands. A newly instituted position of Inspector-General for Recruit Training would oversee both depots. Additionally, the Marine Corps would increase the level of officer supervision of training. All but the latter would be temporary until the Corps had eliminated abuses in the training system.

These ideas, as well as the general contents of the draft statement, originated with Twining but took their final form based upon a consensus of the senior officers at Headquarters Marine Corps, plus key people in Capitol Hill. Twining's method, Hittle remembered, was to compose a draft and then seek advice for improvements. Among those who commented was Russ Blandford, who came over from Capitol Hill to help ensure that the final statement would be palatable to Vinson and the House committee.[32]

One of the key portions of Twining's draft statement was the announcement of the immediate transfer of General Burger from Parris Island. This was an inevitable decision, given the realities of the political climate facing the Marine Corps in Washington, and the continued press attention to Parris Island. Someone had to get the ax, even if it had to be Pate's personal friend, Joe Burger.

At Parris Island, Burger, who apparently had no inkling of impending relief from command, faced a different reality from that of the Marines who dealt with Congress. Burger's reality was the ongoing public relations crisis brought on by almost daily revelations in the press of the widespread problems at the depot.

There was no exchange of ideas between Burger and Twining's working group in Washington. Burger, from his statements to the press, showed no conception of the policies being hammered out in Washington. This ignorance was manifest in a press conference on April 12. Burger said he would not overlook a thing in searching for defects in the recruit training system. This implied that the defects were hard to find, at a time when Twining's draft statement for Pate contained full admission of widespread problems in the system. Burger also said McKeon's case left him "puzzled." This utterance could be construed to indicate confusion within Burger's mind on how to handle the whole affair. The following day Burger admitted that a similar, but nonfatal, night march had occurred in the tidal marshes in 1954. He went on to add that he knew of no such hikes during his own tour. Burger seemed to be advancing the hoary excuse that "It didn't happen on my watch" at the same time that Twining's draft statement contained a straightforward acceptance of Marine Corps responsibility. Burger also figured in the semantic argument among NCOs at Parris Island—as well as in the press——over whether custom allowed NCOs to "discipline" their subordinates or whether they could only "teach discipline." The heart of the argument was the extent of the authority of Marine NCOs. The press stories presented Burger as being at odds with the NCOs and reinforced the largely erroneous picture of Burger as an ineffectual commander. The end result of all these statements and news stories was that Burger inadvertently laid his own neck on the block.[33]

The press was not Burger's only problem. The court of inquiry that was investigating the Ribbon Creek incident soon ran into legal difficulties because of a seniority problem among the affected officers. The colonel who was president of the court realized he might have to call Colonel McKean and others as witnesses. The court notified Burger of the problems inherent in the court questioning officers with greater seniority. Burger, in turn, informed the Commandant, who sent Brigadier General Wallace M. Greene, Jr., the assistant commander of the 2d Marine Division, to Parris Island to complete the inquiry.[34]

Wallace Greene had received his brigadier general's star in February, but, as was customary at the time, had a date of rank of September 1, 1955, the date of the approval of the promotion list. He was born and grew up in Vermont. He graduated from the U.S. Naval Academy (Colonel McKean was a classmate) in 1930. Greene was slight of build, brilliant, and noted for mastering his assignments through long hours of persistent work. In addition, he possessed a forthright manner that quickly attracted the loyalty of subordinates, who felt they had been taken into his confidence.[35]

General Greene wrapped up the court of inquiry on April 20, and forwarded his report to General Burger. Since a military court of inquiry serves roughly the same function as a civilian grand jury, Greene also forwarded the formal charge sheet recommending that Staff Sergeant McKeon be tried by general court-martial. The charge sheet listed four violations of the Uniform Code of Military Justice. These included possession and use of alcoholic beverages in a barracks, oppression of recruits, and drinking in front of a recruit. The most serious charge, which military law broke down into two specific violations of the same article of the code, were manslaughter by culpable negligence and manslaughter while oppressing. Finally, Greene's report recommended disciplinary action against both Technical Sergeant Scarborough and Sergeant King for drinking alcoholic beverages in a barracks.

Lieutenant Colonel Duane L. Faw, the legal officer at Parris Island, reviewed the inquiry report and drafted the forwarding endorsement to the Commandant of the Marine Corps and the Secretary of the Navy. Burger signed the endorsement on April 24, and forwarded it to Headquarters Marine Corps.[36]

Burger's signature on the endorsement destroyed any remaining chances that he could stay on at Parris Island. The sixteen single-spaced typed pages of the forwarding endorsement contained a staunch defense of the existing recruit training establishment. It put Burger on record as recommending no changes in the training system other than a depot order placing all marshes, tidal streams, beaches, and waters out-of-bounds for recruit training, plus a revision of the wording and approach of certain lesson plans at the DI school. This limited course of action was totally at odds with the consensus Twining had reached among the senior generals at Headquarters Marine Corps. Pate's own endorsement, which forwarded the record to the Secretary of the Navy, strongly repudiated Burger's attempt to keep the training system unchanged. Burger would lose his command.[37]

In Washington, General Twining orchestrated the final preparations for Pate's appearance before the House Armed Services

Committee on May 1, 1956. The report of the inquiry would be delivered to the Secretary of the Navy the day before Pate's testimony. That same day, Pate would personally brief both Senator Russell and Representative Vinson about the Corps' plans. Finally, copies of the inquiry report, with all endorsements, would be released to the press at the time of Pate's testimony.

When Twining had the Commandant's statement in final form, he sent Hittle to Capitol Hill to go over the speech with Vinson and Dewey Short. During the meeting, Vinson sat at his desk with Short near him. Other staff members, including Russ Blandford, were present also. When Hittle finished discussing the Corps' proposed actions, everyone present agreed the plan was the best thing to do. Vinson concluded the meeting with his wish to "have the Commandant come over ahead of the hearing for an hour and we'll go over this thing." On May 1 Pate arrived before the hearings began. He sat down with Vinson and Short, and they carefully went through the entire statement.[38]

That same morning, May 1, Hittle also met with Vinson before Pate's appearance. They discussed the statement and Vinson asked, "What do you think of it?" Hittle, who considered the statement a "masterpiece of Twining straightforwardness," replied:

> It's the truth to the extent that we honestly know it now. And I think we know what the truth is in this thing. I can't tell you that it's all the information, but it's everything we know after the Commandant's and his staff's diligent efforts to find out.

Vinson nodded. "That's very good," he said. "That's very good. That satisfies me." Vinson then turned to Hittle, and, with a friendly laugh, said:

> I'm going to have to say something about this. You go on out, get together with Bob [Robert W. Smart, chief counsel for the committee] and Russ, and you write up my remarks right now of what my reaction is going to be after I hear this thing.[39]

When General Pate testified later, he covered all the proposals so carefully worked out with Congress and the generals at Headquarters Marine Corps. Vinson listened as if he were hearing Pate's remarks for the first time. Hittle, sitting in the audience, knew Vinson to be an astute man who always had a purpose for his actions. Vinson, he concluded, had wanted to hear Pate ahead of time so that he would be more familiar with the contents by hearing it twice.[40] By being prepared, Vinson could better control the direction taken by the committee hearing.

When Pate finished, Chairman Vinson was ready. He began by reading from the statement prepared by Hittle, Blandford, and Smart. It outlined the sequence of events following the deaths in Ribbon Creek and praised the Marine Corps' subsequent efforts and its plans for reform. Vinson also praised Pate for the forthright admission of problems at Parris Island. "During my 42 years in the Congress," he continued, "this is the first time within my memory that the senior officer of any Armed Service has had the courage to state in public session that his service could be deficient in some respect." Vinson concluded by saying he believed the Marine Corps should have time to put its own house in order before the committee decided whether a congressional investigation was warranted.

After Vinson finished his statement, he opened the floor to questions. Other members of the committee asked a few innocuous questions before they agreed to give the Marine Corps time to correct the problems at Parris Island. The chairman then instructed Pate to report back to the committee before the end of that session of Congress, at which time they would decide whether to investigate.[41]

Both the Marine Corps and Chairman Vinson had what they wanted. They would continue to work together, and there would be no formal congressional investigation, even though the threat remained real until the reforms planned by Twining were in place and institutionalized.

The following morning, May 2, Colonel McKean read the *New York Times* account of the hearing. To his shock, the story mentioned that he would be among those at Parris Island who would be relieved of their duties. This was the first information about his impending transfer that reached him. This peremptory relief angered him because of the implication of negligence, incompetence, or malfeasance. Additionally, it was an administrative, rather than judicial, action. There could be no appeal. His career would end on this dark note.[42]

General Burger took a more philosophical view of his own relief. He, of course, did not think the move justified and was convinced he could straighten out Parris Island. He accepted, however, that congressional pressure required that something be done. He also agreed that the proposed reorganization was long overdue. Burger, unlike McKean, also had the advantage of private assurances from General Pate that his career would not suffer because of the relief.[43]

There were a few more loose ends to tie up at Headquarters Marine Corps. Pate wanted to have a conference of the general officers on the east coast to explain his rationale and plans for changes in the recruit training system. Colonel Shaw received the assignment to draft Pate's remarks. Later, excerpts from these remarks were printed and distributed as Pate's policy on recruit training.[44]

The remaining major item was the decision regarding the new inspector-general for recruit training and the commanding generals of the new recruit training commands. Twining recommended Major General David M. Shoup for the former position and Brigadier Generals Wallace M. Greene, Jr., and Victor H. Krulak for the latter commands. Before making his decision, Pate discussed the matter with others, including Colonel Shaw. The latter had gone into Pate's office on another errand when the Commandant remarked, "You know, we have got to make a selection for the inspector-general." Pate then named a few possibilities, but noted the problem of breaking anyone loose from his present assignment. Shaw pointed out that Major General Shoup, the stocky Marine officer who received the Medal of Honor for valor on Tarawa, was due to leave his position as fiscal director at Headquarters. Shaw added that the assignment of a Medal of Honor recipient would sit well with both the public and Congress. Further, Shoup was a hard-nosed man who would follow Pate's instructions with great vigor.[45]

General Pate, after considering everyone's advice, decided to assign Shoup to be the inspector-general for recruit training. He did not select the highly regarded Brigadier General Krulak for San Diego, choosing instead to send Brigadier General Alan Shapley, who had gained an impressive record in the World War II Raider battalions.[*] The selectee for Parris Island was the general officer with the most recent experience at the Carolina base, Brigadier General Wallace M. Greene, Jr.

Twining had done his job well, and the Marine Corps had pulled off its coup with Congress. The Corps had gained time to put its own house in order and, by doing so, precluded a congressional investigation of the extent of maltreatment at Parris Island. Twining,

---

[*] Both these officers eventually retired as lieutenant generals.

however, believed that the Corps still would have to pay a heavy price for Pate's mea culpa before Congress. Twining warned the Commandant that the press, deprived of the story of a Marine Corps crucifixion in the Congress, would shift from condemning Sergeant McKeon to supporting him as the underdog in the forthcoming court-martial. Pate did not realize the full implications of that prediction, for he allowed Twining to return to California. When the prediction proved true, Twining was too far away to keep the Commandant on track in the face of mounting press pressure. Pate simply could not withstand it alone. His reactions to the pressures predicted by Twining marked the beginning of a deterioration in the relationship between the two old friends.[46]

4

Instituting
the Changes

Brigadier General Wallace M. Greene, Jr., happened to be at Headquarters Marine Corps when he learned of his appointment as commanding general of the new Recruit Training Command at Parris Island. The orders were a shock, for he already had official orders to an assignment in Washington. In fact, he already had negotiated a lease on a house in Arlington, and was in the Navy Annex to arrange for moving his furniture from Camp Lejeune, North Carolina. He was hurrying up a flight of stairs to the second floor of the building to complete these arrangements when he met General Pate coming down.

"Where are you headed, Wally?" the Commandant asked.

"To report in."

"Don't do that," said General Pate. "I am sending you to Parris Island tomorrow morning to handle the training accident there. Go to the Chief's [the Chief of Staff's] office, read the dispatches, the newspaper reports, and get briefed by the staff. Get ready to leave first thing tomorrow morning by Marine Corps plane. Your family can follow later."[1]

The subsequent whirlwind briefings gave General Greene an insight into the magnitude of the task ahead of him. Consistent with the program devised by Major General Twining, Greene gained authority to introduce any and all innovations he believed necessary. If, after a testing period, these had value to both recruit depots, the inspector-general for recruit training would make them standard requirements. In addition, Greene learned he had the authority to transfer for cause, within twenty-four hours, any Marine officer and enlisted man in his command.

Although these instructions implied sweeping changes, the briefings placed greater emphasis on preserving the essential characteristics of traditional Marine recruit training. There would be no softening of the training program. Existing standards of discipline and physical training were to be maintained. These caveats were critical indicators of the damage-limiting nature of Twining's program. Greene understood and carefully marked these passages in his copies of the briefing documents.[2]

Events moved quickly that second day of May 1956. By that afternoon, General Greene had made his choices for the principal staff officers of his new command, and the personnel department began sending teletype messages to the respective officers' duty stations directing their immediate transfer to Parris Island. The chief of staff of the new training command would be Colonel Robert T. Vance, then with Headquarters Battalion, 2d Marine Division at Camp Lejeune. Colonel Glenn C. Funk, the regimental commander of the 8th Marines, also part of the 2d Marine Division, was Greene's choice to head the Weapons Training Battalion at Parris Island. Greene asked for and received Colonel Richard M. Huizenga, an aviator from the air station at Cherry Point, North Carolina, as his operations officer (G–3). All had served with Greene before, and he valued their abilities and loyalties. All would assume their duties within less than forty-eight hours.[3]

These colonels were key players in Greene's revision of the training system at Parris Island, yet even they were assigned there on a trial basis. They had to prove themselves quickly or face relief from their duties and immediate transfer. Headquarters Marine Corps underscored this status by allowing them to keep their families in their present government quarters for the time being. This provision allowed the men to go to work at Parris Island without the immediate worry of moving their families. At the same time, this meant they could be shipped back from the depot quickly and cheaply should they not perform to Greene's expectations.

The personnel department at Headquarters Marine Corps also began implementing the plans to increase the numbers of drill instructors at Parris Island. The 2d Marine Division, located relatively close to Parris Island, received quotas for qualified technical sergeants, staff sergeants, sergeants, and corporals who would report to drill instructors' school. In addition, the division also had to provide twenty-six regular, unrestricted line lieutenants who would help supervise recruit training at the recruit depot. All were assigned on a trial basis and could retain their family housing at Camp Lejeune for an indefinite period of time.[4]

The following day Brigadier General Greene flew to the air facility at New River, adjacent to Camp Lejeune. At the headquarters of the 2d Division, Greene had a stormy meeting with Major General Reginald H. Ridgely, who was quite angry over the numbers of high-quality officers and men he was losing to Parris Island. Greene, of course, specifically had asked for only two officers from the division, Colonels Vance and Funk. The rest of the reassignments were the work of Headquarters Marine Corps. General Ridgely, however, held Greene responsible and vented his frustration on his former assistant division commander.[5]

General Greene, his aide-de-camp, and six others, left New River at 2:00 P.M. on May 4, 1956, in a Marine transport plane. They landed at the air facility at Beaufort, South Carolina, and proceeded directly to Parris Island.[6]

Greene immediately met with his battalion commanders and, afterward, with Colonel McKean, his Naval Academy classmate. The latter meeting was cool. McKean's previous relief from command affected its tenor, as did the fact that, prior to Greene's recent promotion to brigadier general, he had always been one number junior to McKean on the officers lineal list.

Greene took control of the meeting by reminding McKean that his court of inquiry found that recruits were adequately supervised while at the Weapons Training Battalion. He then expressed regret, "remotely" according to McKean's account, that the latter was being relieved of his command.

"Bill, you know me," emphasized General Greene. "If there had been the least evidence that you either neglected or failed in your duty, I would have clobbered you!"[7]

This ruthless assertion set the tone for Greene's approach to the members of his new command. Wallace Greene meant business. Those who would not or could not perform to his demanding standards did not remain long in the Recruit Training Command.

That afternoon Greene, Vance, and Huizenga met with the more than 600 NCOs involved in recruit training at the depot. Accompanying the three officers were Master Sergeants William G. Ferrigno and Benjamin F. Dutton. The former would be the training command's "field" sergeant major, while Dutton was the "inside" or "office" sergeant major in control of administrative matters. They proved crucial to the success of this meeting with the command's NCOs.[8]

The assembled Marine NCOs listened from their seats while Greene outlined the situation from the perspective of the Commandant and Congress. He carefully described the measures he was implementing to carry out his assignment to eliminate maltreatment while preserving the character of boot camp. Next, in a remarkably democratic step for a Marine officer, he bluntly asked the NCOs what they wished to do: to help him or oppose him.

General Greene recalled:

> There was a very obvious undercurrent of opposition on the part of the younger NCOs and a stronger position of support by the senior DIs—support openly and with emphasis advocated by Ferrigno and Dutton. After a period of conversation and debate among themselves, those present were asked what they wished to do—and the consensus was to throw their lot in with me and to back the new plan and regime.
>
> I then promised them two things: (1) no lowering of standards in recruit training, and (2) a betterment of conditions under which DIs worked.[9]

The drill instructors then received a chance to comment on problems at the depot. They wanted smaller platoons and the authority to impose minor punishments on recalcitrants, especially those slow learners in the lower mental groups. The assembled Marines also desired a lengthening of boot camp to allow more time for training. Some saw a need for an official definition of hazing as well as a reduction of pressure upon drill instructors. Others voiced complaints that battalion commanders too often let off recruit offenders rather than impose nonjudicial punishment. The DIs requested assurances they would not be court-martialed because of recruits' perjured testimony. A major complaint centered on the drill instructors' living conditions.[10]

Giving the DIs the opportunity to air their complaints and to make recommendations proved a major step in the institutional response to Ribbon Creek. Greene and his staff had not had time to hammer out a complete program for reform. Prior to this meeting they could speak only in generalities; even Greene's earlier meeting that day with his battalion commanders served primarily to impress them with the fact he was truly in command. This subsequent meeting with the DIs brought out fundamental problems, which defined much of the reform program Greene initiated, as well as giving him the support of his NCOs.

General Greene consolidated NCO support by convening a Staff NCO Advisory Council, composed of himself and the senior NCOs of the training command. The council met the next day, a Sunday afternoon, and thereafter, following a name change to DI Advisory Council, became a standard feature of Greene's leadership method at Parris Island. It was, he recalled later, a practice he observed throughout his career. He considered the council an invaluable tool, which fostered a sense of unity, trust, support, and loyalty between the commander and his senior enlisted Marines. As such, he believed the council absolutety essential to attaining his goals at the Recruit Training Command.[11]

The first meeting of the DI Advisory Council produced many of the same recommendations made at the larger gathering the previous day. The council members emphasized some new points, however. First, they believed a DI must have some opportunity to both reward and punish his platoon. The senior NCOs also strongly recommended adoption of a better form of headgear to protect DIs from the broiling Carolina sun. The khaki barracks cap had a bill but did not protect the neck. The soft khaki garrison cap did not even have a bill to shade the eyes. The green herringbone twill cap worn with the field uniform was also inadequate in the summer sun. The senior NCOs suggested the wide-brimmed pith helmet, which had served Parris Island well in World War II.

The NCOs also discussed training problems. For example, platoons lost nearly half their scheduled close-order drill time to necessary activities such at dental appointments. They also cited a need for better liaison between the recruit training battalions and the Weapons Training Battalion while platoons were at the rifle range.[12]

These meetings of the council provided practical information to the leadership of the training command, helped shape the scope of the reform effort, and produced better morale among those involved in recruit training. As one depot staff officer noted, the ability to listen to subordinates made General Greene an excellent choice for the job. Greene, he recalled, "didn't get excited, he had some good ideas, but he would listen to his staff, he listened to other people; he may not agree with you but he would listen . . . he evaluated their ideas when he made his final decision."[13]

Meeting and talking with subordinates served, of course, for two-way communications. As Greene informed Major General Shoup, he worked through the council for the ultimate goal of getting the DIs to police themselves and stop problems before they grew into general court-martial cases.[14]

On Monday, May 7, 1956, the Recruit Training Command's boss made his first telephone report to Shoup. They discussed the training command's immediate needs, plans, and initial actions. Greene planned to establish a special inspection section, which would keep tabs on the training program. His staff already had begun writing up the procedures guiding the section. However, Greene also wanted more vehicles, for the inspection section as well as for his whole command. Greene cited a need for a qualified public affairs officer to handle the numerous newsmen who came to report on Marine recruit training. The items already accomplished included Colonel Funk's assumption of command of the weapons battalion that day. In addition, the training command would have its own staff duty officer and officer of the day starting that night. Greene also announced his decision to abolish the traditional "skinhead" recruit haircut in favor of a modified "crew cut."

Shoup was not wasting time in his new assignment either. He too was getting a firm grip on his responsibilities as inspector-general for recruit training. He informed Greene he would make his first inspection trip to Parris Island the following day. His airplane would arrive at the air station at Beaufort at 8:30 A.M.[15]

The following morning, while Shoup conferred with the new depot commander, Major General Homer H. Litzenberg, Greene bade farewell to the ill-fated Platoon 71. The platoon had completed its recruit training and was departing for the Infantry Training Regiment at Camp Lejeune. Greene stood in front of the assembled platoon and removed the rank insignia from the collar of his summer tropical khaki shirt, a gesture that had considerable morale-building potential among Marines at the depot. Then, as he remembered later, he said roughly the following:

> I am talking to you as one Marine to another—not as an officer to a recruit—but as an older Marine to a younger Marine, both of whom share the heritage and traditions of a truly great organization.
>
> Unfortunately, during your entrance into our Corps, and through no fault of your own, you were involved in a training accident which resulted in the death of six of your comrades.
>
> In spite of this misfortune, by successfully graduating today from recruit training, you have demonstrated your abilities and shown your loyalty to the Marine Corps when the going was really tough.
>
> It is now up to each of you as you leave to carry on this record and show the rest of the Marine Corps and the world you deserve the title of United States Marine!—and I believe you will![16]

Shoup arrived at Greene's office later that morning, and the two Marines talked for just over an hour before Shoup departed for Washington. A long conversation was not necessary for them to have a meeting of the minds. Greene had known the burly Medal of Honor holder for many years, going back to prewar service in the 1930s with the 4th Marines in China. On Saipan during World War II, Shoup, as the 2d Marine Division's chief of staff, worked closely with Greene, the division's G–3 (Operations) officer. They even shared the same foxhole one night during a Japanese *banzai* attack. The two generals were old friends, now sharing the dangers of still another "battle."[17]

Shoup got down to business quickly. He emphasized that it was vital to retain the fundamental nature of recruit training because he believed it crucial for victory on the next battlefield. Shoup complimented Greene for making satisfactory progress in only a few short days. Finally, he said that Headquarters Marine Corps planned to send out several thousand questionnaires to major Marine bases to find out what enlisted Marines thought of boot camp.[18]

Back in Washington, General Shoup continued his energetic efforts to guide the changes at the two recruit depots and to push their requests through the Headquarters bureaucracy. Following Greene's example, he met with former drill instructors assigned to Headquarters, and notified both depots of the results. A key suggestion that came out of the meeting was for issuing additional uniforms to DIs.[19]

Shoup continued the preparations for sending out questionnaires as part of a Corps-wide survey on recruit training. A knowledge of changes in recruit training over the past decades, Shoup thought, would help him solve the current problems. He specifically wanted to know more about the DIs' use of improper methods, especially corporal punishment and verbal abuse. Such data, should it prove physical abuse was a recent phenomenon in boot camp, would be helpful in overcoming any Marine's opposition to the changes being made at the two depots. Should the data indicate otherwise, Shoup could merely file the results away.

The personnel director at Headquarters Marine Corps allowed Shoup to use the people and facilities of the Procedures Analysis Branch in designing the questionnaire and analyzing the results. The branch tested the questionnaire on about 1,000 Marines stationed in the Washington area. Then, on May 18, it sent out 27,000 question-naires (rather than the 50,000 originally considered), distributed among twenty-seven major commands. As the various commands returned the completed forms, over 100 officers set to work to analyze the responses (See chap. 1, above, for results of the survey). However, not until July, in the midst of Staff Sergeant McKeon's court-martial, would Shoup have the final results.[20]

Wallace Greene was facing a different kind of question at Parris Island, one that seemed to be trying to raise doubts about his new programs at the depot. It came from a newspaper article by Bem Price, one of the top feature writers for the Associated Press. Though Price's text contained a balanced account of the changes at Parris Island, as well as the reaction to them by some drill instructors, the article provided enough negative material to upset the training command's staff, not to mention General Greene himself.

The article's very title, " 'Book' Is Sad Story to Marine Noncoms," implied Greene was a martinet who did things "by the book." To most veterans of the citizen army of World War II, this was not a compliment, to say the least. Additionally, Price wrote that Greene, like Pate, had "spent most of his time in the Corps in staff jobs." This statement carried a devastating innuendo among Marines, who value service "with the troops."

Price's article also noted that some drill instructors referred to the ten captains in Lieutenant Colonel Richard L. Sullivan's new inspection section as "sneaky petes" or spies. The article seemed to link the creation of the inspection section to the arrival of 116 DI school students who, some feared, had been sent as replacements following wholesale courts-martial for drill instructors. Price even quoted two Marines who grumbled over their beers at the Staff NCO Club. One reportedly growled, "We've had the old Corps, the new Corps, and now this fouled-up thing." The other one complained, "We get more like the Army every day."[21]

Price's article also presented a more positive side to the training changes. He noted that Greene had ordered the transfer from the recruit battalions of all those who were "noneffective." In addition, training officers no longer suffered under burdensome additional duties. Moreover, the inspectors had orders not to get between a DI and his platoon, but to discuss any training problems with the senior officer present from the respective company or battalion. Greene himself was quoted as saying, "I have no intentions of changing this system or letting it get soft."[22]

The emotionally charged atmosphere at Parris Island amplified the negative aspects of Price's article at the expense of the more positive material. This was dangerous for both General Greene and the Marine Corps. If the attitudes of Parris Island's Marines polarized against Greene's reforms, or of those Marines lost their respect for Greene's advocacy of training by leadership rather than fists, then the whole program might falter. This was critical, for the Marine Corps' position with Congress remained delicate and a full-scale investigation of Parris Island's abuses might well have cost the Corps the chance to preserve its training system and put its own house in order.

The Price article angered Wallace Greene, who considered it an attack on both him and his reforms. On his own copy he underlined the portions he found most objectionable. Thereafter he kept a personal file containing Price's subsequent feature stories about Marine training. In the months to come, the contents of this file would grow in significance to the history of the Ribbon Creek affair.[23]

Bem Price was not the only one digging deep into the drill instructors' problems. The staff of the training command, particularly Master Sergeant Ferrigno, worked hard to uncover drill instructor concerns. Ferrigno listened to DIs' complaints and, when necessary, gave a short lesson on leadership and the obligations of Marine NCOs. He also kept his commanding general informed of legitimate gripes. Commissioned officers on the staff were just as active. The senior officers went so far as to attend the NCOs' social functions whenever possible, as a means of making obvious the command's interest in the drill instructors' welfare.[24]

By early June the drill instructors had tangible evidence of the command's concern. Each DI had received the right to an unlimited amount of laundry at Marine Corps expense. In an era when starched khakis were the uniform of the day, a DI now could maintain his sharp appearance simply by changing into a fresh uniform if the starch wilted in the steamy Parris Island weather.[25]

A total of eighty-seven unmarried drill instructors moved out of the recruit barracks, where they had lived so long, and into specially refurbished DI quarters. General Shoup had pried money loose from Headquarters Marine Corps to renovate and furnish an unused bachelor officers quarters (BOQ) at Page Field, the deactivated airfield on Parris Island. With these funds the depot requisitioned the necessary furniture and mattresses for the building, which contained its own dining facility. These new quarters got the bachelor DIs away from the recruit environment on nonduty evenings, and allowed them to relax in surroundings enjoyed only by commissioned officers or senior Staff NCOs elsewhere in the Marine Corps.[26]

The new bachelor quarters did not alleviate the serious shortage of housing for the influx of married Marines. The base itself had few quarters for these families. Off-base housing also was scarce because of the presence of a large number of civilian construction workers who were upgrading Beaufort's World War II temporary air station into a permanent facility. One sergeant, Greene reported, had to struggle financially to keep his wife and baby in a house in Beaufort, which could only be described as "an unsatisfactory tenement." The dismal housing situation even lowered the motivation of married students at DI school, which cost Greene sorely needed personnel. In response, Major General Litzenberg, the depot commander, requisitioned 200 air-conditioned house trailers. He also asked Washington to defer two major air conditioning projects at the base and to use these funds to renovate another building at Page Field. By mid-July both projects were well underway.[27]

These concerns for the welfare of the drill instructors extended into a study of the DIs themselves. The Recruit Training Command (RTC) staff sifted through hundreds of personnel records to determine the characteristics of the Marines engaged in training recruits. They found the average DI's pay grade was 4.7, which in 1956 meant he was either a senior sergeant (pay grade E–4) or a junior staff sergeant (pay grade E–5). His IQ, based upon General Classification Test scores, was 107.7, slightly above the "average" of 100. He had 10.6 years of education and 7 years and 11 months of active service. His total time as a DI averaged 13.5 months. Of all the drill instructors, 56 percent were married; of these, 65 percent had children. World War II veterans comprised 26 percent of the total; 63 percent had served in Korea.[28]

Members of Shoup's own personal staff also came to Parris Island to delve into the drill instructors' thoughts and concerns. One study, by Captain Mark P. Fennessy, who spent several days at the depot, found the majority of the DIs pleased with the command's efforts to improve their living and working conditions. In addition, he noted a distinct difference in approach between younger and older instructors. Younger, less-experienced Marines were more likely to take an

"I will not put up with it" attitude toward recruit mistakes. Older men tended to say: "You don't have to mistreat a person to make him learn."

Several DIs told Fennessy that peer pressure caused much of the problems with maltreatment. There was a tendency among many drill instructors to consider a man a good DI only if he were "shouting, pushing, and just generally raising cain at all times." Finally, Captain Fennessy found many DIs believed the training should be made more physically demanding.[29] In the latter respect, help was on the way in the form of a new physical training program.

Despite its reputation for rugged training, the level of physical conditioning achieved by Marine recruits prior to the establishment of the Recruit Training Command had not been very high. In fact, the Infantry Training Regiment at Camp Lejeune had to institute its own physical training program so that Parris Island's graduates would have the stamina to complete the Individual Combat Training course.

At Parris Island, physical conditioning had been within the purview of the DIs, whose approach varied with their individual athletic ability. Too often they considered organized athletic games, such as baseball or football, to be sufficient. However, only the athletically inclined recruits tended to participate in the games, while the rest sat on the sidelines.[30]

Colonel Huizenga, who had responsibility for the overall training program, assigned First Lieutenant Neil S. Wheelwright to develop a new physical conditioning program. Wheelwright, who had majored in physical education in college, used the Army field manual on physical training, FM 21–20, as a guide in designing a program of graduated difficulty for recruits. He then assembled a group of Marine athletes who became his instructors. The new program began on June 19, 1956.

Lieutenant Wheelwright's new system included an initial strength test during the first week of training. This served as both a base point for judging individual progress and a means for identifying those youths not yet ready to undertake rigorous exercise. Thereafter, recruit platoons began each day with a morning run, supplemented with a fifty-minute physical training period later in the day. These morning runs and exercise periods gradually increased in distance and intensity to match the recruits' growing levels of endurance. There were additional tests in the ninth and twelfth weeks. Recruits ran the obstacle course in the eighth week and, to teach teamwork, lifted heavy logs in the ninth week. On the last night before graduation, platoons went to the Depot Sports Center for an introduction to the recreational facilities available on most Marine bases.

The new physical training program was a major success and became a mandatory part of any visitor's itinerary. One writer claimed it gave the depot "the air of an Olympic village." General Greene, who was personally committed to physical fitness, was just as enthusiastic. In one personal letter to General Shoup, he wrote in part:

> I want to tell you again, Dave, that the effect of this physical training program is almost beyond measurement. . . . The enthusiasm that overflows from this program is being felt throughout the entire schedule. The recruits are getting heavy tans and getting into excellent physical condition. . . . But even more important . . . is the unlocking of group spirit and the developing of teamwork which is so necessary to a Marine. The rate of petty offenses and disciplinary problems has dropped off. The DIs and officers are just as enthusiastic about this program as are the recruits.[31]

Not all recruits could meet the demands of the physical training (PT) program and wound up in the newly organized Special Training Company's conditioning platoon for the weak and the overweight. Because of the different needs of these two types of men, the company eventually organized a strength platoon for the weak, and a conditioning platoon for overweight recruits. If, after thirty days of exercise and a balanced diet, these men could not meet the standards of the initial strength test, they went before an aptitude board for consideration for discharge from the Marine Corps.

The Special Training Company also included two other platoons. The hospital platoon handled those returning from hospitalization or awaiting medical discharge. The motivation platoon received anyone unable or unwilling to give his maximum effort in the normal training environment. These were the recruits considered "quitters" or sociopathic nonconformists. Removing them from regular platoons was one of the new methods for reducing DI frustration and, at the same time, the maltreatment rate. Recruits assigned to the hospital and motivation platoons remained until they became fully fit to participate in normal training or until discharged from the Marine Corps.[32]

The threat of assignment to the Special Training Company, especially to the motivation platoon, became powerful negative incentives for recruits to give their best at all times. New recruits quickly learned that if the regular training were rough, training in the special platoons was far worse. The platoons for the weak and overweight devoted much of each day to strenuous physical activity and exercise. The motivation platoon, feared partly because of the stigma attached to those who did not really want to be Marines, used specially selected DIs, psychiatrists, forced self-examination, and other psychological devices, as well as demanding physical challenges, to engender self-respect, acceptance of authority, and the desire to complete boot camp and become a Marine. Assignment to any of the special platoons meant that a recruit would be set back in his training and have to spend a longer time at Parris Island.

The Recruit Training Command also instituted some positive incentives for recruits. Prior to the completion of the rifle range, recruits wore a bronze Marine Corps emblem on their helmet liners. Thereafter, they wore a gilt emblem, signifying "senior" recruits.[*] Those whose performance dropped off could lose the right to wear the emblem. As Greene informed Shoup, ". . . when a man loses his ornament, he automatically becomes the focus point for group pressure and he is soon trying to win it back."[33]

Each platoon carried a guidon showing its platoon number. Since the guidon bearer marched in front of the platoon, his job became highly prized. The guidon itself became a group incentive, since the DIs could take it away if the entire platoon's performance dropped. A bare staff—or a guidon rolled up and tied around the staff—became a badge of group dishonor, and platoons fought to retrieve the right to carry their guidon.[34]

Other innovations appeared, some to become institutionalized, others to be dropped after a short testing period. One that lasted was the painting of the recruits' helmet liners with aluminum paint to reflect the fierce Carolina sun and reduce the incidence of sunstroke. On the other hand, Greene exerimented with and, after two months, discarded the practice of using troop handlers rather than DIs during a platoon's initial forming phase. The purpose of the experiment was to reduce the pressures on his drill instructors. He dropped the practice after discovering the DIs preferred the old method.

---

[*] This practice apparently did not last long. It definitely disappeared prior to 1959, when I first arrived at Parris Island. Apparently, too many Marines believed the wearing of their emblem was a right to be earned along with the title "Marine." Both were to be bestowed only at recruit graduation.

The training command also tried using a brief ceremony in which the battalion commander turned over a new platoon to its team of drill instructors. This included a formal presentation of the platoon's guidon, a part sometimes played by Greene himself. This ceremony became something of a show, and the DI Advisory Council informed the training command that DIs were griping because too many of the "brass" attended the ceremony. The ceremony soon disappeared.

The command also dropped the "honor platoon" system in an effort to reduce pressure on the DIs by eliminating a source of intense competition among them. This practice, however, reappeared some months later when the command decided that a certain amount of competition among platoons was desirable.[35]

While many of these minor innovations were simply a matter of the commanding general making a decision, the larger ones were not. They cost money, a scarce commodity in the years of the Eisenhower administration's "Second New Look" in defense spending, which placed the Marine Corps under severe fiscal constraints. New obstacle courses, athletic uniforms for the new PT program, renovations to buildings, house trailers, and other items all cost hard dollars. Any increases in personnel or funding for recruit training had to come out of the hide of another major command, a fact not likely to please any of their commanding generals. Parris Island had to compete with these other commands for people and money, and the voice of a very junior brigadier general did not carry much weight in such competition.

Brigadier General Greene, of course, had General Pate's promises of anything needed to shape up Parris Island. However, it took the drive and influence of David M. Shoup to shake loose people and money from Headquarters Marine Corps. Shoup was the buffer between Greene and the Headquarters staff, which had the difficult job of balancing the whole range of the Corps' requirements. Shoup had the advantage of being at Headquarters, and could exert influence on a face-to-face basis while distant commands had to rely on letters, messages, and telephone calls. In addition, Shoup did not hesitate to go directly to the chief of staff if the respective Headquarters staff sections were not forthcoming. David Shoup got results quickly—then often wrote a quick note to "Wally" on Greene's original letter and immediately returned it to Parris Island.[36]

Some of Shoup's efforts on Parris Island's behalf increased the work load of other commands, another factor that caused resistance among the Headquarters staff officers. For example, because of

Shoup's intervention on behalf of Parris Island, some other Marine base had to provide marksmanship coaches for temporary duty during the summer at the Naval Academy rifle range. In addition, Camp Lejeune had to readjust its schedules and facilities to handle the training of Marine Reserve units originally slated for Parris Island.[37]

The problem of acquiring large numbers of highly qualified NCOs to attend the DI school ultimately proved virtually insoluble even for David Shoup. Both Shoup and the Headquarters staff tried hard to meet the depot's needs. On May 2, 1956, in the initial enthusiasm to get the training commands set up, Major General Edward W. Snedeker, the G–3 at Headquarters, prepared letters for Pate's signature directing all major commands to end the practice of sending nonqualified NCOs to DI school. The letters stressed the importance the Commandant placed on the proper selection of NCOs for this duty. By late May, however, Snedeker was protesting the increasing numbers of students requested by the depots. In a note to Lieutenant General Vernon E. Megee, the chief of staff of Headquarters, Snedeker wrote, "Inasmuch as there is not an inexhaustible supply of the 'finest NCOs in the Corps,' we should husband our resources somewhat." On July 12 Major General Robert O. Bare, the director of personnel, notified Shoup he was finding it very difficult to fill all the quotas for prospective drill instructors. Bare said he had instructed his enlisted assignment section to waive the obligated service and IQ requirements for DI school when considered "in the best interests of the Marine Corps." Shoup could only forward a copy of Bare's memo with an attached note to "Wally." "Obviously the situation is tight," he wrote. "Do all you can not to have too many DIs."[38]

General Greene, upon receiving Shoup's note, quickly drafted a reply saying flatly the director of personnel's plan would only increase the attrition rate at DI school. Further, he said he believed there were sufficient qualified NCOs in the Marine Corps to meet the quotas for 150 students for the remaining two classes scheduled in 1956.[39]

In essence Greene took the position that he would not lower his criteria for drill instructors. It was an impasse for which there was no real solution. In Washington, Shoup could only continue to lobby for the assignment of the best possible NCOs to the recruit depots.

Officer assignments were just as troublesome. The establishment of the Recruit Training Command resulted in the quick transfer of numerous officers, both into and out of Parris Island. Some, such as Colonel Henry W. Buse, Jr., who retired years later as a lieutenant general, received transfers from Parris Island simply because there was a general housecleaning following Ribbon Creek. Few commands wanted the officers whom General Greene relieved for cause; neither did they wish to lose the "younger, forceful, talented" officers needed to fill the many vacancies at Parris Island. In addition to transfers, there were quick retirements by some officers at Parris Island because they simply did not want to make the effort to conform to the new pressures at the base. These retirees also had to be replaced by top-quality personnel, such as Colonel George H. Cloud, who became the depot's supply officer after his orders to Camp Lejeune abruptly changed. In addition, Greene demanded and, with Shoup's backing, received some choice in which officers came to his command for duty as battalion commanders. The resolution of all these prickly matters fell to the director of personnel and his staff at Headquarters Marine Corps.[40]

Major General Shoup and his assistants acted as more than advocates in Washington. They also served as a clearing house or go-between in the effort to achieve uniformity between the training and policies followed at the two recruit depots. Uniformity, however, was not always possible. For example, the more benign climate at San Diego gave that base a distinct advantage over subtropical Parris Island. The latter, for illustration, had to take far more elaborate precautions against heat casualties, and, as a consequence, lost a certain amount of training time.

Each base eventually adopted some policies of the other, including some with which it had at first disagreed. San Diego tried and then dropped the use of a special platoon for recruits with motivation problems. The DIs had quickly nicknamed it the "goon platoon," a term deplored by the officers. However, San Diego later set up a unit similar to Parris Island's Special Training Company. Parris Island, on the other hand, adopted Brigadier General Shapley's policy of providing unlimited free laundry to selected personnel other than DIs. These included the special-subjects instructors, DI school instructors, and troop handlers at the receiving barracks. At San Diego, these totaled less than forty additional men. In Shapley's opinion, the extension of free laundry prevented an undesirable division among his NCOs at a time of intense upheaval and change in recruit training.[41]

The extent of the changes in the administration of recruit training had been both dramatic and extensive. These modifications were not the result of half-baked ideas, but represented thorough considerations of cause and effect. For example, the increased around-the-clock officer supervision had decreased the traditional autonomy of the drill instructors. In response, the training command enhanced their position and prestige through better housing, additional free uniforms, and unlimited free laundry. The final step in enhancing the DIs' prestige was the introduction of the pre-World War II campaign or field hat as the symbol of Marine drill instructors.

At the first meeting of the DI Advisory Council in early May, General Greene had noted the request for improved "head gear" for DIs. Further study, and the advocacy of Master Sergeant Ferrigno, settled on the field hat as the item most preferred by DIs.* It shaded the neck and eyes well, but did not keep the head as cool as the pith helmet. The field hat was a bit of tradition going back to the "Old Corps" of pre-World War II days. It also was more suitable for year-round wear than the pith helmet.

By early June, the depot had requisitioned 1,000 field hats for delivery on September 1, 1956. This was not soon enough for Wallace Greene. He wrote General Shoup on June 14, asking that Headquarters Marine Corps allocate some of its uncommitted funds from the final quarter of the fiscal year, which ended on June 30. He wanted to order 700 hats immediately from the J. B. Stetson Company.[42] He got the money.

The crew of a Marine transport aircraft picked up the hats at the factory on Friday, July 20, 1956, and flew them to the Beaufort air station. At 7:30 the following morning, all 603 drill instructors of the Recruit Training Command obtained their new hats.

The issuing of the new hats provided an example of masterful political timing. The DIs received their new hats just at the point in Staff Sergeant McKeon's court-martial when DIs were being subpoenaed and having to testify. It came in the middle of massive media attention to the trial and to Parris Island. Photographs of the DIs wearing their field hats in a mass formation received wide exposure in the press. The National Broadcasting Company filmed

---

* The pith helmet was a practical alternative for wear in the Carolina summer. It was cool, and its wide brim provided good shade for the eyes and neck. It later became the hat used by marksmanship instructors at the rifle range.

a television segment that appeared on a then-novel "coast-to-coast" news program the following Monday morning. *Life* magazine also picked up the story. Greene characterized the effect of the new hats as "terrific," and wrote Shoup that it had provided a big boost for the DIs.[43]

The new hats had a symbolism far beyond that of a badge of office for Marine drill instructors. They also symbolized a break with Parris Island's past, and the introduction of a new way of training recruits. Thus the Marine Corps could point to the Ribbon Creek incident as an irrelevant anachronism. As Staff Sergeant McKeon's court-martial began that July, he had, from the Corps' point of view, only historical significance. An era had passed.

5

The McKeon
Court-Martial

The court-martial of Staff Sergeant Matthew McKeon[1] demonstrates that an institution's efforts to strengthen its position in one area can weaken it in another; however, such a newly created "weakness" can have positive long-term benefits for the institution. For example, immediately after the Ribbon Creek incident, the Marine Corps exercised considerable political skill in convincing Congress to allow the Corps to put its own house in order. The Marines then quickly organized their ad hoc program for revising Marine recruit training and managed, through prodigious effort, to institute the reforms prior to McKeon's court-martial. These reforms allowed the prosecution of Matthew McKeon without the Marine Corps having to rationalize in court the defects of its previous training system. This fact strengthened the Corps' institutional position, but weakened the ability to prosecute McKeon.

The Corps, by effectively repudiating its traditional training system, allowed McKeon's defense to turn the tables and become the defender of that system and, by extension, of traditional Marine virtues. This approach enabled the defense to draw upon the reservoir of good will the American public held toward its Marine Corps. Further, these defense tactics permitted the defense counsel to bring in not only a famous Marine hero, Lieutenant General Louis B. "Chesty" Puller, but also General Pate himself as defense witnesses. Yet, even in surrendering the courtroom initiative to the defense, the Marine Corps benefited, because this defense victory erased any lingering public image of a vengeful Marine Corps out to destroy one of its own. In the end, McKeon's defense counsel also defended the Corps.

Suspicions of the Corps' intentions toward Staff Sergeant McKeon arose soon after the tragedy. Following General Pate's initial news conference at Parris Island on April 9, the day after the tragedy, many Americans suspected McKeon would not receive a fair trial. A group of NCOs at Headquarters Marine Corps even went so far as to begin collecting money for McKeon's defense. Their interest quickly waned, however, after later revelations, substantiated by telephone calls to senior NCOs at Parris Island, indicated McKeon had been drinking on duty prior to the ill-fated march.[2]

A group of former Marines in Washington, D.C., began efforts in McKeon's behalf. Their movement originated during the court of inquiry, when a news story published a statement by a former Marine, Charles J. Stefano, defending McKeon's right to discipline his men. Stefano soon received some sixty telephone calls from people who agreed with him. In response he called a meeting on April 18, 1956, which about twenty veterans attended. Some claimed to have known McKeon personally from their Marine Corps service and, of these, three volunteered to testify as character witnesses for the accused sergeant.[3]

At Parris Island numerous enlisted Marines harbored misgivings about the forthcoming trial. Many considered the deaths the result of a training accident. They felt let down by senior officers' statements that McKeon (and, by extension, other NCOs) had no authority to order such a disciplinary march. Additionally, Pate's presumed advocacy of a court-martial as a means of punishing McKeon to the fullest extent created a wall of resentment at the training base.[4]

None of these stirrings was as significant to Staff Sergeant McKeon's future as the informal committee formed on his behalf in New York. Two state supreme court judges, James B. M. McNally and Walter A. Lynch, organized the group from among prominent lawyers with a known commitment to protecting civil liberties. Among the lawyers contacted by Justice McNally was one who claimed he feared the trial could become another Dreyfus case. This concern caused him to answer McNally's telephone query with: "I'll not only join the committee—I'll try the case."[5]

The new volunteer defense counsel was Emile Zola Berman, a specialist in civil suits and, at the time, unknown to the public. His immigrant parents, both of whom were committed the cause of civil liberties worldwide, had named him after Emile Zola, whose thunderous "J'Accuse!" had been so critical to the defense of Captain Dreyfus against the French Army. Berman did not look distinguished; one writer described him as having "the forbidding look of an oddball. He is a skinny little man of 53, with a small, bald head, big ears, and a long, sharp nose." Berman was, however, a brilliant, highly respected trial lawyer whom other lawyers came to observe at work presenting a tough case to a jury. In addition he possessed a magnetic personality and courtly manners that made even strangers quickly forget his appearance.[6]

Berman won many cases through detailed preparation and a masterful ability in presenting evidence. "Most lawyers," he once told a reporter, "think you only have to present the evidence. . . . That's nonsense. The important thing is how you present it and how you analyze it."[7]

Berman's courtroom skills with evidence won a case in 1956 in which the victim received $350,000 from New York City. It was the largest award ever made against the city at that time. A widow, Mrs. Clara Levine, had been struck by a police car and left crippled for life. Berman won by demonstrating that the driver of the police car had a clear and unobstructed view for a block before he struck Mrs. Levine.[8]

Staff Sergeant McKeon and his family welcomed Berman's help. Thomas P. Costello, McKeon's brother-in-law, who was himself a lawyer and who defended the sergeant during the court of inquiry, recommended acceptance of Berman's offer to serve as chief defense counsel without charge.

As McKeon's chief defense counsel, Berman approached the trial in a manner that gave his side the initiative. By keeping himself one step ahead of the prosecution, he managed to control events from the very beginning. He managed to do so because the Marine Corps, including its prosecuting officer, took a narrow view that focused on the trial itself. Berman, however, took the broader approach that the courtroom trial was only one step in a complex legal process. The latter included the various forms of automatic review of the court-martial verdict and sentence required by the Uniform Code of Military Justice. Berman also perceived that public opinion could be as important in the ultimate resolution of McKeon's case as the evidence presented in court.

Berman began his orchestration of McKeon's defense the day after he became the chief defense counsel. He appeared on Dave Garroway's nationally televised "Today" show. Berman announced during the interview that he had been retained without any agreement regarding a fee, a statement likely to help shift public opinion in favor of the defense. He raised the Dreyfus analogy by saying he was defending McKeon out of a feeling that there were broader issues involved above the mere fact of the drownings. Berman continued that he wanted to ensure that these issues were adequately presented in court.[9]

Berman's appearance on the "Today" show was an astute piece of pretrial stagecraft. The analogy to the Dreyfus case was weak, yet the mere mention of that famous French case would ensure that the Marine Corps bent over backward to ensure a fair trial. In addition, his on-camera statement about wider issues being involved served to tap the wellspring of Marine Corps paranoia. Lieutenant Colonel Duane Faw, the legal officer at Parris Island, saw the statement as a preview of Berman's tactics in the forthcoming trial. Faw expected Berman to attempt to shift the blame from McKeon to the Marine Corps itself, to put the institution on trial. Faw was not the only one who took this view. A few days later, on May 1, General Pate's statement before the House Armed Services Committee also contained the declaration that the Marine Corps was on trial.[10]

Major General Merrill Twining, who prepared Pate's statement, knew of Berman's reputation as a lawyer. As soon as the announcement came about Berman being the new defense counsel, Colonel Hittle called some prominent lawyer friends in New York City. "Boy, he's a sharp one," they replied.[11]

Berman was too smart to allow a rush to try Staff Sergeant McKeon. When Secretary of the Navy Charles S. Thomas issued the appointing order for the court-martial, which set the trial date for May 14, Berman quickly requested a delay. He pleaded for time to clear up his existing schedule and for preparing the defense. The secretary agreed and set the new date at July 14, a Saturday.[12]

The defense team, as it prepared for the trial, kept the Marine Corps off balance. In fact, the Marine Corps found itself whipsawed by Berman's tactics. The senior Marine generals feared the outcome of the court-martial would be to place the Corps itself on trial. On the other hand, they could not counter Berman's tactics lest they be accused of prejudicing the case, thus raising the Dreyfus specter.[13]

Berman fed their fears. On May 9, in a letter to the Secretary of the Navy, he asked for the names and civilian addresses of all Marines, excluding psychiatric cases, discharged from Parris Island within the year.[14] This request seemed confirmation of the Corps' worst apprehensions.

These Marine worries worked to Berman's advantage in his dealings with General Pate. Ultimately, they helped Berman separate Pate from his advisers and brought the Commandant into the defense counsel's camp, where he agreed to testify for the accused at the court-martial.

Berman began his campaign for Pate's aid soon after becoming McKeon's counsel. Pate's personal staff officers knew Berman wished to meet with the Commandant. They strongly recommended Pate not do so. At first he took their advice. Soon, however, Berman managed to convince Pate over the telephone that there was no harm in an unofficial meeting. Pate acquiesced and told his staff he would be visiting relatives in Norfolk for the weekend.[15]

Colonels Hittle and Simpson suspected the real purpose of the Norfolk trip. They went in to Pate's office and said, "If you go down there, under no circumstances meet with Berman." Pate asserted he had no intention of doing so.[16]

The meeting took place, nevertheless, and Berman's charm and personality won over the Commandant. The latter volunteered to testify for the defense at McKeon's trial.[17] When Pate agreed to testify, Berman had won one of the key victories in his defense of Staff Sergeant McKeon.

As the trial date drew near, Parris Island began making its preparations. For example, the depot commander recommended that the Commandant end the policy of having boot-camp graduates go on leave and then return to Parris Island before going on to Camp Lejeune for Individual Combat Training. The new plan would send them to Camp Lejeune for their additional training before their "boot leave" The ostensible reason was to give them their infantry training while they were still at "peak proficiency." The depot commander's letter, however, went on to say the depot did not want large numbers of recruit graduates on board the base where they would be engaged in relatively unsupervised work details during the McKeon trial. If continued, these details, called "police duty," would provide reporters wide access to too many young Marines who might inadvertently reveal too many unsavory details about pre-Ribbon Creek recruit training.[18]

Around the same time, Lieutenant Colonel Faw, at the request of the depot chief of staff, prepared an assessment of anticipated defense tactics. Faw, of course, still believed the defense would attempt to save McKeon by indicting the Marine Corps. Much depended, he wrote, on the ability of the prosecutor and members of the court to keep out "irrelevant matters." He went on to discuss his expectations of the way Berman would oppose each of the charges against Sergeant McKeon.[19] Faw's memo soon proved to have been nothing more than an academic exercise.

The Secretary of the Navy had been the official who issued the appointing order for the court-martial, which gave him responsibility for conducting the trial, not the depot commander. The depot's own responsibility therefore involved only the provision of logistical support for the trial.

The precise nature of depot support soon came into question, particularly regarding public relations. On July 6 Lieutenant Colonel Donald R. Nugent telephoned from Washington to advise the Parris Island command that he was the Headquarters Marine Corps action officer for the trial. As such, he expected to come to Parris Island for the trial and to handle briefings for the press. However, that same day, Major Charles B. Sevier notified the depot commander that, as the prosecuting officer appointed by the Secretary of the Navy, the establishment of policies for handling the press during the court-martial was his own responsibility. Faced with these conflicting demands, the depot could only request clarification from Headquarters Marine Corps.[20]

The staff at Headquarters was not very clear on the procedures required by the situation either. A July 10th teletype message from Headquarters limited the recruit depot to clerical and logistical support for the trial. This included provision of a courtroom, preparation of the trial record, and facilities for the newsmen covering the trial. The message also directed the depot commander not to communicate directly with the Secretary of the Navy about these services. Instead, he was to go through either the prosecutor or the Commandant of the Marine Corps, meaning the Headquarters staff.[21]

The following day, after further staff deliberation in Washington, Headquarters sent additional instructions to Parris Island. The new message advised General Litzenberg it was temporarily assigning Lieutenant Colonel Nugent to the depot for the duration of the trial. He would bring copies of press packages previously released on May 1, the date of Pate's testimony before the House Armed Services Committee. These materials could be given to the press, but without comment or interpretation.

The message from Headquarters Marine Corps also contained highly detailed instructions on the release of information about the trial and its participants. The message had all the trappings of a gag rule for Marines at Parris Island.[22]

Rumors quickly circulated among the base's Marines that the new depot chief of staff, Colonel Harvey C. Tshirgi, had convened all his top staff officers for a meeting on relations with the press during the trial. Marines heard they could not be forced by reporters to make any comment on the trial or any other subject. Further, any unauthorized conversations with a reporter could be a violation of the Uniform Code of Military Justice, Article 37, which prohibits attempts to influence the action of a court-martial.

These rumors gained credence when the depot released and widely distributed an undated mimeographed sheet entitled "News Release Policy from CMC." The sheet paraphrased the Headquarters message of July 11, with a final admonition: "Read Article 37, UCMJ."[23]

These rumors and instructions made Marines at the base unwilling to talk to reporters. The command's motivation for this extreme policy may have stemmed from one or more reasons, including distrust of the press, the desire to ensure a fair trial for Staff Sergeant McKeon, or an urge to protect depot Marines from any court-martial for remarks that might influence McKeon's trial.

Regardless of the reason, the inevitable effect was to close practically all sources of information available to reporters except trial testimony and statements from Emile Berman. The policy could not have been more in Berman's favor if he had written it himself.

Another tactical advantage enjoyed by Berman was his continuing contacts with General Pate. Berman used their growing relationship for immediate gains as well as for achieving his long-range goals for McKeon's defense. An example of the immediate value of this friendship occurred on Friday afternoon, July 13, before the trial actually convened. The occasion was a pretrial conference of the judge, the law officer, and the opposing counsel. Whether by Berman's design or coincidence, the meeting had hardly begun before being interrupted by a messenger who said Berman had a long-distance telephone call from the Commandant. The meeting recessed for seventeen minutes while Berman went to another room to confer with Pate over the telephone. When the meeting reconvened, there was no mention of the nature of the conversation, However, such an extended conference between the Commandant of the Marine Corps and the accused's defense counsel could only have disturbed the trial's principals.[24]

Planned or not, Pate's telephone call fitted into the pattern or strategy Berman followed in defending McKeon. One element of his strategy was an effort to change the American Public's negative image of Matthew McKeon. With this in mind, Berman arranged for newsmen to interview McKeon at home with his family and then photograph the Marine playing with his new baby. One of the reporters involved said afterward, "I was sure McKeon was a first-class son-of-a-bitch. Now I say you couldn't ask for a nicer guy."[25]

The subsequent news stories created the desired shift in public opinion. People who had earlier considered McKeon a barbaric monster became sympathetic. The American public began to believe McKeon's intentions had been good, but he had made a grave error in taking the platoon into the marsh at night.[26]

Marine opinion was not overlooked in this campaign. Berman gave reporters details of his own distinguished war record as an Army Air Force intelligence officer, which defused any thoughts of his being antimilitary. He engaged in light banter with the Marine officers involved in the trial, as well as with Marines in the audience. He let it be known that he worked on his case each night until 3:00 A.M., then he showed up at the courtroom each morning alert, cheerful, and wearing a freshly pressed suit. Each day the courtroom quickly became quite uncomfortable because of the Carolina heat and humidity, yet the Marines in their tropical shirts could see Berman steadfastly refusing even to remove his coat.

One Marine officer noted:

> The hit he made in the trial was amazing. To look at that fellow, you'd think he was opposed to everything we stand for. But he talked to us in our own language, and it was Berman, not the prosecutors, who defended the Marine Corps' traditions. I don't know of another civilian who understands the military mind as well as he does.[27]

This officer's remarks disclosed the irony of the McKeon court-martial. Before it began, the Marine Corps had assumed Berman would try to put the Corps itself on trial. He did just the opposite. He became the protector of the Marine Corps training system (and generated newspaper headlines to that effect), and maneuvered the Corps into appearing bent on attacking its own methods. This upset the prosecution's preconceived notions about how to try the case.

Berman had the prosecution off guard and kept it that way. For example, he publicly appealed for witnesses who would testify about previous night marches into the tidal areas around Parris Island. He then had McKeon's wife and several attractive women

Marines filmed for television as they answered the many incoming calls from potential witnesses. However, he never used these volunteers as witnesses during the trial. On another occasion, he demanded that the Marine Corps provide him with the statistical results of the survey on recruit training recently conducted by Headquarters Marine Corps. He said it might contain information useful to McKeon's defense. He received the report, but never used it in court. The real effect of such tactics was to permit him to retain the initiative in the trial and to force the prosecution to keep preparing for courtroom battles that never materialized.[28]

The virtual gag rule against Marines talking with the press gave Berman almost a monopoly on all information beyond courtroom testimony. He used that monopoly exceedingly well:

> Out of court Berman was considerably less restrained. . . . Every afternoon when court adjourned he lolled around in his small, crowded room at the nearby Bachelor Officers Quarters 905, stripped down to his underwear, pouring Scotch for reporters, wisecracking about the day's events and providing them with usable material that did Sergeant McKeon no harm.
> Unlike the other cell-like BOQ rooms at Parris Island, Berman's was equipped with an air conditioning unit and a well-stocked refrigerator.
> It was a pleasant place to spend an hour.[29]

On Friday, July 20, at the end of the trial's first week, Berman requested that the following day's session be short. He explained there was an important matter that required his attention. He did not mention that the matter in question was another meeting with Pate in Norfolk. There the two men sat on the porch of Pate's relatives' home and had a long conversation in which Berman convinced the Commandant to testify.

Berman later said he used a simple, direct approach to get Pate to agree. "I told the general," he recalled, "that it was the only way to get himself and the Marine Corps out of this jam.[30]

The following Monday morning, Pate's staff learned of the meeting and the outcome. They believed the Commandant did not have to testify. In fact, they considered it a bad idea.

Colonels Shaw and Simpson tried to talk Pate out of testifying at the trial. Shaw remembered: ". . . the two of us were in front of him there at his desk, trying to persuade him . . . and he lost his temper and said, 'This Parris Island Business, I don't want either one of you to talk to me anymore about it.' "[31]

That week McKeon's trial proceeded routinely. Few Marines at Parris Island, including Brigadier General Greene, learned that Pate would be coming to the base to testify as a defense witness. On Wednesday, July 25, Greene even wrote in a letter to Major General Shoup that newsmen were "becoming hard-pressed to find material for stories. Unless something develops between now and this weekend, I believe that most of the feature writers will take their departure, leaving only the wire services to cover the trial."[32]

As July ended, the prosecution rested its case and Berman began presenting his carefully-crafted defense. Part of the plan involved McKeon taking the stand to testify in his own behalf. When he testified, the "taut, strained" Marine said at one point that he considered Platoon 71's discipline to have been poor and admitted he had halfheartedly slapped three recruits. Major Sevier, the prosecutor, asked in cross-examination: "Was that the way you maintained discipline, by slapping recruits?"

McKeon replied: "There was no meanness in my heart, no hate . . . when I slapped those men. . . . I'd be in the back of the platoon and if they were goofing off, I'd give them a little belt beside the head."[33]

Pate arrived at Parris Island for the afternoon session that same day, August 1, which was the twelfth day of the trial. Bem Price, the Associated Press's top reporter covering the trial, was astounded when Pate entered the courtroom, strode over to Staff Sergeant McKeon, and shook his hand.

"I am here to help you in every legal way," Pate said. "Good luck to you, boy." Pate then turned and headed to the witness chair.[34]

Pate's testimony was equally astounding, especially since he had earlier relieved Burger ostensibly for not being sufficiently punitive in the case. He said under oath that he did not think the night march, "apart from the results," constituted "oppression" of the recruits. He admitted that prior to the Ribbon Creek tragedy officer supervision had slipped a bit. Perhaps his most headline-making statement was that if he had been in charge at Parris Island at the time of the incident, his response would have been to reduce McKeon by one rank and transfer him for stupidity.[35]

The following day Berman pulled another coup by calling retired Lieutenant General Louis B. "Chesty" Puller as a defense witness. Puller, whose heroism under fire had earned him five awards of the Navy Cross, the second highest award for valor in the naval service, virtually had the stature of a Homeric hero among Marines. Berman called him to the stand to testify as an expert on Marine training. General Puller said that good discipline was vital to military victory. However, he conceded under cross-examination that good leadership precluded placing subordinates in a hazardous situation without reconnaissance and good cause. Perhaps his most important contribution for the defense—and the following day's newspaper headlines—was to say, "I think from the testimony of General Pate yesterday that he agrees and regrets that the Marine Corps ever ordered this man be tried."[36]

Meanwhile, in Washington, Pate's appearance at the trial was causing considerable turmoil. Colonel Hittle, the congressional liaison officer, received a number of calls from incensed members of Congress demanding an explanation of Pate's action. This was a delicate issue, because only congressional expectations that Pate would clean up the Parris Island mess had precluded a full-scale investigation of Marine recruit training. Should Congress lose faith in the Commandant, an investigation was still possible. Hittle was careful in his reply to these queries: "The Commandant said what he did because he thought it was the right thing to say. And he's bending over backwards not to prejudice the case for McKeon."[37]

The greater question within the Navy Department was the possible effect of Pate's testimony on the trial verdict and the subsequent review process. The legally ticklish part was the reality that Pate was in the chain of command that would decide whether to uphold or reduce any sentence imposed by the court. There was a real danger that the Navy Department and the Marine Corps might be charged with exercising "command influence" over the court's decision. If so, this could very well lead to the court's verdict being overturned on appeal. Under Secretary of the Navy Thomas S. Gates quickly released a statement saying that Pate's testimony should not necessarily affect the court's verdict or sentence.[38]

Berman disagreed. He abruptly rested his case the day after Puller's testimony, a week earlier than he originally planned. He had fought the prosecution every step of the way. He had made requests and demands that kept the prosecution off guard and unsure of the direction the defense case would follow. Berman had argued firmly in court over points of law, yet carefully courted Marine opinion and sensibilities. He had called eleven defense witnesses, including the two generals and a Navy physician who diagnosed McKeon's back problem as a herniated spinal disk. The latter did much to bolster the defense's contention that on April 8 McKeon's judgment had been affected in part by acute pain. There were still thirty-three drill instructors standing by to testify as defense witnesses about other marches in the tidal marshes around the island. Yet, with the two generals' testimony in the record, Berman abandoned the idea of calling the DIs to the stand. He believed the two Marine generals' testimony would have a positive effect on the court, and he decided to quit while he was ahead. Berman rested his case and confided to the press: "If I can't go with two generals, what could I do with a bunch of drill instructors?"[39]

He did not mention another point in his favor: his surprise move would catch the prosecution off guard again, and force Major Sevier to make his closing remarks off-the-cuff, while Berman was well prepared with a carefully crafted summation of the evidence. He retained the court-room initiative.

On August 4, 1956, the court found Staff Sergeant McKeon guilty of only simple negligence and drinking on duty. The sentence, however, was stiff. The court sentenced him to receive a bad conduct discharge, to forfeit $30 per month for nine months while confined at hard labor, and reduction to the rank of private.

When the court-martial record reached Headquarters Marine Corps during the review process, Major General Robert E. Hogaboom, acting in the absence of both Generals Pate and Megee, signed off on a recommended course of action for the Secretary of the Navy. He based his recommendations upon material that Major General Twining had left behind expressly for that purpose. The secretary followed that advice.

On October 5, 1956, Secretary Thomas voided the bad conduct discharge and the fine. This was a logical move, given the relatively minor nature of the offenses of which the court found McKeon guilty. Secretary Thomas also reduced the period of confinement to three months and let stand the reduction to private. The action was both fair and politically sound. It put to rest any potential for critics to raise the Dreyfus analogy and, at the same time, indicated the existence of a compassionate naval service. Buttressing the latter was the Secretary's statement giving McKeon "the opportunity to build for himself a useful and honorable career."[40]

During the period following the court's decision on August 4 and the Secretary's review on October 5, Matthew McKeon had continued to spend his off-duty hours at home, even though he was technically in confinement. With three weeks off his sentence for "good behavior," he had to spend only twelve days in the brig following the Secretary's review. Private McKeon left the brig on Saturday, October 20, 1956. On Sunday night, McKeon flew to New York at Berman's expense where the latter hosted a "victory dinner" at Toots Shor's renowned night club.[41]

When he returned to Parris Island, Private McKeon requested he not be transferred from the base until he found out whether a motion picture would be made of the Ribbon Creek affair. The movie apparently was supposed to resemble *The Caine Mutiny*. Berman was handling the details of the negotiations for McKeon. McKeon said that, once this matter was settled, he wanted an assignment with a Marine aviation unit, preferably in Japan.[42] There would be no movie, however, and the former staff sergeant soon departed Parris Island for the Marine air station at Cherry Point, North Carolina.

Matthew McKeon's involvement with Parris Island and Marine recruit training ended quietly. His legacy of upheaval within the Marine Corps continued.

6

Making the Changes Work

The end of the McKeon court-martial and Private McKeon's departure from Parris Island did not end the problems of the Recruit Training Command. The new system of administering training was in place before the trial, but Brigadier General Wallace Greene and his training command still faced staggering obstacles for the full institutionalization of that system. The first of these centered on the fact that the system was not without its flaws. Experience with it quickly brought out the need for additional alterations and refinements. In addition, the separate but interrelated responsibilities of General Greene and the depot commander created inevitable frictions. Worse, the passage of time after the trial saw an erosion of the give-them-anything-they-want attitude at Headquarters Marine Corps in Washington.

The continued incidence of maltreatment remained a concern for those trying to reshape the program. It also concerned the recruits who endured it. Richard H. Bradford, who later became a professor of history, provided some examples of the ongoing abuses. On the day the DIs took control of Bradford's platoon, one of them threw a recruit to the ground. A Navy officer witnessed the incident and brought charges. There was no court-martial because the recruit denied the DI had done anything to him.

There were other incidents that day, which no officer witnessed. Bradford, who was wearing a helmet liner, was hit on the head several times by blows delivered with a swagger stick. Such things went on in the platoon throughout their stay at Parris Island.

Bradford also witnessed an extreme case of hazing, an incident that he said was unique in his experiences as a recruit.* The story

---

*A member of this writer's platoon received a box of candy from home. One DI made him smoke cigarettes, eat candy, and drink warm water until he vomited. This, however, unlike Richard Bradford's story, took place in the head (latrine) and the

centered on another recruit, a misfit whom the DIs several times found engaged in unauthorized cigarette-smoking.

> One Sunday afternoon when the Senior DI was demonstrating how to make a field transport pack, [Sergeant] C——— was given charge of [Private] T———. He put him on a table and made him smoke half a dozen cigarettes at once. . . . Then C——— made him drink warm water until he vomited in his canteen cup. Then he made him drink his puke! All this time the rest of the platoon was quite aware of what was going on, and once in a while C——— would carry on a Peter Lorre–Sydney Greenstreet humor with the head DI.
> "Is this bothering you, Gunny?"
> "No, it is music to my ears."[1]

Such treatment, though inexcusable, stemmed in part from one of the faults in the philosophy of the Marine recruit training system. The DIs were expected to modify the lifelong behavior of misfits—"rotten apples" and "dead-end kids." It was an unreasonable assignment, one for which neither the DIs nor anyone else had the skills and qualifications. Eventually, as happened to the man described above, the recruit would wind up in the brig and receive either an undesirable or a bad-conduct discharge. Not until after the Vietnam War did the Marine Corps adopt the policy of returning misfits to civilian life quickly so that the DIs' time would not be taken up with handling the untrainable.

Such drastic changes were not acceptable in 1956. At that time refinements to the training program, though time-consuming, were evolutionary by nature rather than revolutionary. For example, the training command established its "Instruction-Inspection Section" prior to McKeon's court-martial, but did not publish the section's standing operating procedures (SOP) until July 26, after the trial had begun.

The SOP ensured the retention of control of training procedures by General Greene's staff while, at the same time, strictly observing the traditional command courtesies. These courtesies included the requirement that each member of the section check in and out with the respective battalion headquarters before and after each inspection of a recruit platoon. For that reason no battalion commander

---

recruit was allowed to vomit into a toilet. Bradford's DI took the method to the ultimate extreme. Note, however, that both cases involved *hazing* rather than the use of fists, which was so prevalent in the pre-Ribbon Creek era.

could complain of lack of knowledge of the activities of observers from his parent headquarters.[2]

The training command staff examined all phases of the recruit regimen with a view toward improvements, especially in those areas that posed hazards to the lives of recruits. The effects of the humid, subtropical summers at Parris Island posed one such threat. In 1951 there had been 350 cases of heat exhaustion and 25 cases of sunstroke. Two of these recruits died. In the early summer of 1952, at the height of the Korean War, the depot changed its hot-weather procedures after suffering 388 heat-related cases and 1 death. These modifications reduced the number of such problems considerably; however, another recruit died in 1953. There had not been any deaths in either 1954 or 1955.

The newly established Recruit Training Command did not want more deaths from any cause in 1956 and published new instructions for training during the hot weather occurring between May and the middle of October. During these months, all newly arrived recruits were given time to adapt to local climatic conditions before taking strenuous physical workouts. Further, the command regulated all physical activity through a system of colored flags that indicated the meteorological conditions of heat and humidity. When the flag pole carried a yellow flag, recruits in their first three weeks of training could not perform strenuous activities. A red flag stopped all such training for everyone.[3]

A concurrent project reviewed the standard, approved lesson plans used to train recruits at Parris Island. Such reviews are periodically necessary, for the trainees need to receive the latest information related to service regulations, weapons, tactics, and doctrine. The revised lesson plans, however, contained elements that illustrate the mood of the American military—as well as the nation itself—during the mid-1950s. The Marine Corps, a professional institution theoretically separated from national politics, embarked upon a program in peacetime of political indoctrination of its new recruits.[4]

This indoctrination program, which melded with the new physical training program, had its origins during the Korean War, which had ended three years earlier. That war, especially during its early phases, demonstrated the military reality that "poor physical condition and lack of stamina of the individuals could prove disastrous to the unit." The source of that poor conditioning appeared to many Marines to be the supposed softness of American youth due to "modern living."[5]

The national dismay, after the Korean War, at the reports of "collaboration" by American prisoners of war with their Communist captors seemed another manifestation of the weaknesses of the nation's young people. Many professional officers saw military service as the ideal way to overcome the perceived deficiencies in the younger generation, including the supposed lack of ideological, moral, and physical "discipline."[6]

Captain F. S. Thomas, writing in the professional journal *U.S. Naval Institute Proceedings,* stated this belief:

> It is futile to castigate society for failure to indoctrinate American youth properly. It is equally futile to state unequivocally that since home, school, and community have not provided the adequate training, it is not within the province of the military to do so. It is our province to protect our country, and if we must expend additional allotments of our time and public funds to further refine the new material with which to protect it, then the very essence of our professional honor and the nature of our public trust demands that we do so.[7]

During the 1950s many American adults, having endured the rigors of the Great Depression, had little respect for the nation's adolescents. These youngsters, they complained, had never lived under trying conditions and took comfort for granted. In the same vein, the military services were not entirely happy with having to make do with citizen-soldiers who were either drafted or, despite Marine Corps rhetoric about being a volunteer service, had enlisted because of the draft. These young men considered their military service not as an honored, lifelong calling, or even a short maturing experience, but simply a temporary diversion in their personal lives.[8]

Despite such complaints, the draft-motivated enlistees of the 1950s possessed characteristics that have always existed in American citizen armies and which are vital to the continued existence of a democratic society. Captain Thomas's article, while written to describe deficiencies in American youth, enunciated this fact. He wrote:

> As means of communication have improved in our civilian society and as living has gradually assumed a more technical aspect, recruits

exposed to these influences have become more critical in their attitudes and feel competent to inquire into causes and effects and to search for explanations.[9]

To correct these perceived deficiencies, the political indoctrination lectures at Parris Island included the history of the United States and an "objective" study of totalitarianism and Communism. The content of this series of classes delved into the "application of true democracy to the individual." Since the United States is a representative rather than a true or pure democracy, the classes appear to have taught concepts as fuzzy as the recruits supposedly had. In addition, some of the rhetoric included clichés purloined from the far left and the far right, such as the one that characterized the period as one of "daily ideological struggle."[10]

The effort to improve the recruits as American citizens spilled over into the area of religion and dining etiquette. In addition to mandatory attendance at church services, the training command required the recruits to say a prayer at each meal. Every table in the recruit mess halls had a plastic-covered card bearing several prayers.

When eight men had arrived at the table, the last man gave the order: "Seats!" The men sat down in unison, and the last man at the table said grace from the card. The recruits then ate while sitting erect and keeping their arms and elbows off the table. The idea was to teach them to eat in a manner vaguely similar to that expected of a "gentleman" and thus enhance the view that they had come up in the world by joining the Marines.[11]

Neither political nor religious indoctrination, however, was among the primary concerns of the young men undergoing training at Parris Island. When they filled out their confidential recruit questionnaires in the third and tenth weeks of training, they consistently cited the need for more and better food. (Their second desire was to be convinced that the training was still "tough"!)[12]

These recruit complaints surfaced in July 1956. General Greene, however, had made a practice of constant inspections of the food served the trainees and knew the quantity had not decreased. The source of the complaints was obvious to him. The new physical training program was increasing the recruits' appetites, especially after the third week of training when the required effort jumped to the next higher level.

General Greene ordered "seconds" lines set up in each recruit mess hall, and requested a study of the caloric content of meals at the base. The depot's food service director reported that the average caloric level for each day in July was 4,742. The highest level, 5,366 calories, occurred with the holiday meal on July 4; the low was 3,982 on July 16. While these totals may have been adequate prior to the new physical training program, the latter's requirement for a morning run, an hour of heavy exercise, and considerable marching throughout each day demanded the food intake jump by approximately 1,000 calories a day. The recruits simply were not getting enough food; their bodies craved more.[13]

Both the depot and the training command worked together to stretch their "food dollars" as far as possible. With the advice of food service personnel from San Diego, the depot managed to increase the milk ration to one quart per recruit per day. Food service managers also readjusted the distribution of their authorized food allowance to provide a more balanced flow of calories to the recruits.[14]

The exchange of information between San Diego and Parris Island was a notable feature of the months following the Ribbon Creek incident. The two depots compared their own accomplishments with each other, with the realization that Headquarters Marine Corps was doing the same.

One of the comparisons between the two depots that disturbed General Greene was the consistently lower rifle qualification scores at Parris Island. He asked Colonel Glenn Funk to investigate.

Funk, the new commander of the Weapons Training Battalion, was familiar with conditions under which recruits on both coasts fired for qualification. Those from San Diego went to Camp Matthews, just north of the city.* The mild Mediterranean-type climate of southern California provided a far more comfortable environment for shooting than that which the recruits endured at Parris Island. Funk's report, however, touched on another aspect of range scores. He noted that he considered the qualification rate (81.3 percent over the previous twelve weeks) to be about right. Funk said he did not believe higher scores were possible without cheating. Funk also added that when a command put emphasis on getting higher scores,

---

* The campus of the University of California, San Diego, now occupies the site of Camp Matthews.

people cheat in order to give the commander what he wants. The implication of cheating at San Diego was clear in the report, which also warned, again by implication, that cheating would occur at Parris Island if the command applied pressure to raise scores. Greene recognized the validity of the argument, filed Funk's memorandum, and concentrated on more pressing problems.[15]

The drill instructors remained a primary concern for Greene. When he arrived, there were no black drill instructors, a fact he quickly changed, along with his other efforts to increase the number of drill instructors. Nevertheless, despite the increased number of DIs, their work loads remained heavy. Their normal work day lasted from 6:30 A.M. to 5:30 P.M. Every three or four nights, depending upon the number of instructors with a platoon, a DI took his turn as the duty drill instructor and slept in a room in the recruit barracks. His duties required him to stay awake until around midnight completing paper work related to the platoon. In addition, he normally had to get out of bed at least once between midnight and reveille to ensure that the recruit on fire watch remained alert.*

These hours, the pressures of the job, and the strong devotion to duty of most of the men could combine to wreak havoc with their personal lives. Marriages suffered, and some even disintegrated, simply because the men spent most of their time with their recruits.[16]

Greene and his staff, with the assistance of General Litzenberg, continued their efforts to relieve the pressures on their instructors. The new DI quarters at Page Field, plus another at the main station, provided bachelor DIs, regardless of rank, with living conditions that only Staff NCOs or officers enjoyed at other Marine bases. In addition, each DI received four extra sets of summer uniforms and enjoyed free laundry and dry cleaning. Greene and his staff kept abreast of DI concerns through constant inspections of training as well as the advice from the DI Advisory Council.

This body, which grew out of the Staff NCO Advisory Council, consisted of the command sergeant major, the sergeants major of each recruit training battalion, and the senior instructor from the DI

---

* A series of recruits pulled one-hour stints during the night for the combined purposes of training and safety. Such watches were mandatory in the tinder-dry wooden barracks left over from the World War II era. The fire watch also prevented theft of equipment and made sure the DI awakened on time in the morning.

school. It met frequently. Its members also had direct access to General Greene, so that minor problems could be eliminated before they became major.[17]

The curriculum of the DI school changed little. The primary alteration was a stricter screening of the students by the depot psychiatrist. The lack of major change at the school stemmed from the command's approach to the relationship between drill instructors and recruits. The training command made no attempt to alter the traditional relationship. Even the "shock treatment," which formed the very core of the recruit experience, remained untouched by the post-Ribbon Creek reforms. Other than the strenuous but more even-handed physical training program, recruit training remained virtually unchanged in its initial traumatic impact on the recruits themselves. The transition from civilian to Marine remained a memorable experience. In fact, Ribbon Creek's primary effect on the recruit training system, despite the wailing of many Marines, was to provide what Parris Island had wanted for years: more officers and more drill instructors.[18]

Greene's reforms also did not alter many drill instructors' attitudes toward recruits. They continued to view recruits as "boys" who had to be changed into "men." Most DIs believed that grabbing a "boy" by his collar and shaking him up a bit should not be considered maltreatment. They preferred this method to that of threatening charges under the Uniform Code of Military Justice. Article 15 of the Code, as then written, gave battalion commanders with the rank of major and above the authority to impose minor punishments upon offenders or to order courts-martial for more serious cases. DIs, however, stood by their belief that it was better to shake up a young man than to put a permanent mark against his record.[19]

This attitude provided the rationalization for many DIs to slip back into their old training routines—maltreatment, assault, and illegal financial dealings. Their attitudes and practices ran head-on into the increased level of officer supervision. The number of courts-martial for DIs increased after late August 1956, when there were no trials pending. By mid-September there were ten cases on the court-martial docket. To the shock of many DIs on the island, those convicted were receiving stiffer sentences than McKeon himself, and for far less severe offenses. Greene tried to reduce the number of courts by taking summary action in each case where possible, with the goal of keeping these incidents out of the newspapers. He largely succeeded, despite a few stories reaching the press via worried mothers and other relatives.[20]

The training command vigorously investigated each allegation of wrongdoing, both to protect the innocent DI from trumped-up charges and to punish the guilty. There were three levels of investigations. The first was a rather cursory check designed to eliminate mere rumor. The second went into the complaints actually raised by recruits. If the allegations were false, the command prosecuted the recruits who raised them. When the command determined a DI might have actually committed an offense, it conducted a formal pretrial investigation as required by the Uniform Code of Military Justice. The final step was the court-martial itself. [21]

It was at the level of the pretrial investigation of serious offenses that the Recruit Training Command lost control of the legal process. Minor offenses, of course, could be handled through nonjudicial punishment by commanding officers. The courts-martial, however, came under the jurisdiction of the depot commander, not the training command. This system, established under the Commandant's order creating the Recruit Training Command, in essence gave the depot commander the primary responsibility for discipline and created tension between the two commands.

The case that brought this tension to a head was not related to maltreatment but to the scope of a DI's authority. It illustrates the Recruit Training Command's primary concern of preserving Marine recruit training rather than weakening it, as some critics charged.

On October 6, 1956, a drill instructor ordered a recruit to double-time around the parade ground for making mistakes during close-order drill. The recruit refused. On October 9 a summary court-martial (one officer acting as a magistrate) convicted the recruit of disobedience of a lawful order. The court sentenced the man to fifteen days confinement at hard labor and a $25.00 fine. However, the depot's law officer recommended to General Litzenberg that the findings and sentence of the court be set aside. The law officer's rationale was that the Uniform Code of Military Justice did not allow NCOs to order "punishment" such as double-timing. Only commanding officers, the law officer argued, could authorize punishment.[22]

Colonel Robert Vance, the chief of staff of the training command, believed strongly that it could not let the law officer's recommendation go unchallenged. Vance wrote a memorandum to Greene outlining the issues raised by the case. If the law officer's opinion were allowed to stand, he noted, it would hit at the heart of recruit training. Specifically, it would weaken the authority of drill instructors (to say nothing of NCOs throughout the Marine Corps) to the point that it would be impossible to conduct traditional recruit training.

General Greene agreed, for he believed there was a distinction between "corrective action" and "punishment." This distinction had to be made, especially for recruits who were still changing from civilian to military life, and who had not yet acquired the habit of instant obedience to commands. With this in mind, he had his staff gather the pertinent documents that would accompany a letter to Litzenberg. The letter, which justified his position in detail, said in part:

> Throughout military history, the official view of the mistakes of a recruit, even in the most harsh military systems, has been to consider them not as offenses against the existing code, whatever its nature, but evidence of undesirable habits to be replaced by new habits inculcated in a regular teaching process. The teaching process in military training centers . . . has always included various physical means of conditioning mind and muscle in a new pattern of habits. The conditioning methods authorized by this command are directly related to training itself, are military in nature, and are restricted to those functions of prescribed drill and physical exercise which, when administered with common sense, will neither harm the individual nor personally degrade him.
>
> Examples of these functions are double-time, manual of arms, push-ups, and other elements of the prescribed physical training routine.[23]

Greene's arguments had a validity that extended beyond recruit training, for they touched upon the authority of all Marine NCOs. Wallace Greene believed that "corrective action" had to remain a part of recruit training. If NCOs could not mete out minor punishments, even under the euphemism of "additional instruction," than commissioned officers would have to assume the functions of NCOs.

Greene decided the evidence so obviously supported his position that a formal letter to Litzenberg was unnecessary. He raised the issue in a discussion with Litzenberg, and the two Marine generals quickly agreed on the necessity of protecting the authority of the DIs and other Marine NCOs. This settled the issue, and the draft letter and its accompanying documents went into Greene's personal files, bearing his notation, "Not sent—discussed w/ Litzenberg 071400 January 57 [2:00 P.M., January 7, 1957].[24]

Wallace Greene's disagreements with Headquarters Marine Corps were not so easily resolved. The basic problem was cost; the new training initiatives, especially the two-week extension of recruit training, were expensive in both time and money. Major General Edward F. Snedeker, the Headquarters G–3, had argued against the extension from the beginning. As early as May 25, 1956, he advised the Commandant that around May 1957 the extension would be decreasing the number of men available for the Fleet Marine Force by over 13,000. He predicted that even a year later, after the personnel pipeline began flowing more smoothly, the combat forces might still have a deficit of almost 10,000 Marines. He suggested it might be necessary for the Marine Corps to deactivate certain units and man its Pacific units at the 90-percent level.[25]

These recommendations meant the Marine Corps might have to revise its policy of concentrating its personnel in the Fleet Marine Force. Such a revision would have a major effect on every aspect of planning by Headquarters Marine Corps. Concerned over the costs of the new recruit training program, the G–3 in September 1956 asked the two depots to access the value of the longer training schedule.

Greene recognized this as a threat to his program and fought its implication through his advocate in Washington, General Shoup. Greene pointed out to Shoup the higher quality Marine being produced under the twelve-week system, as well as the reduced pressure it imposed upon both recruits and DIs. He argued further that if the Marine Corps ever had to accept larger numbers of men in the lower mental categories (Mental Group IV), it would take the entire twelve weeks to train them. The clincher to his argument, however, was that the twelve-week program had been widely advertised as a corrective measure following Ribbon Creek. Greene cautioned that the Marine Corps was still "living on the side of a volcano" as far as the possibility of another incident triggering a congressional investigation. Shoup agreed, and, with his backing and advocacy, Greene's arguments prevailed—at least for the time being.[26]

Headquarters Marine Corps did balk at some other portions of Greene's program, especially the purchase of additional training equipment. Greene wanted $61,600 for physical training items, plus $64,284 for such things as two new parade fields, obstacle courses, and classrooms. In addition, between May and September, the training command had spent $184,070 for DIs' fringe benefits such as free laundry, clothing, and quarters, as well as $2,726 for transportation.[27]

When Greene found Washington reluctant to allocate additional funds, he turned to Litzenberg. The latter managed to "find" $45,000 in his budget to spruce up building AS–33 at the old air station as another new DI quarters. However, the project could not start until title to the building shifted from the Navy's Bureau of Aeronautics to the Marine Corps. By late September, with the number of new drill instructors still increasing at the depot, Greene again appealed to Shoup, this time for help in expediting the title transfer.[28]

General Greene also turned to Litzenberg for money to buy more athletic equipment to meet the needs of the new physical training program. He recommended the purchase be made not from funds derived from congressional appropriations, but from "non-appropriated funds" obtained from the profits of the base's post exchange system. He justified the expenditure with the rationale that the new physical training program's basic objective was to "foster an inclination on the part of each recruit to maintain his own physical fitness by taking advantage of athletic recreation facilities available to him in the Marine Corps."[29]

Such recreational facilities relied upon post exchange profits for meeting their operating expenses. Greene, however, was stretching a point in trying to link recruit physical training with off-duty, recreational-type physical training.

Greene was not asking for minor amounts of money from the exchange profits. The training command wanted enough money to buy sufficient sets of barbells, with 100 pounds of weights each, to supply each recruit platoon with a set for use during the platoon's hour of "free time" each night. A more pressing need was for new tumbling mats for the expanded judo training. The old mats were inadequate, as evidenced by the numerous injuries sustained during falls. The training command also wanted to provide judo outfits to the judo instructors, plus appropriate outfits for the physical training instructors. Both groups were then supplying their own, which produced justifiable complaints.[30]

The depot's recreational council, which oversaw the expenditure of the post exchange's profits, disapproved the training command's request on two occasions. General Litzenberg then bucked the request up to the Commandant in early November because of recent instructions that required the Commandant's approval of all major expenditures. Within two weeks, Headquarters itself had provided the necessary funds. The judo mats, however, were slow in arriving.[31]

Throughout these early fights to obtain the means to carry out the new training initiatives, Greene could rely on the support of Major General Shoup. That support continued even after Shoup became the Inspector-General of the Marine Corps in September 1956. Nevertheless, the abolition of the post of Inspector-General for Recruit Training, combined with the frequent travel Shoup's new duties required, left General Greene more on his own. Gradually, Greene's correspondence shifted to direct communications with General Pate. By January 1957 Greene was no longer sheltered by the umbrella of Shoup's influence, for the latter had assumed command of the 1st Marine Division at Camp Pendleton, California. This adversely affected Greene's ability to win the bureaucratic battles with Headquarters Marine Corps.

In the spring of 1956, immediately after Ribbon Creek, the two recruit training commands could obtain all the officers they needed. This was no longer true by January 1957, which resulted in the deactivation of one of the recruit training battalion headquarters at Parris Island. In addition, the G–1 (Personnel) at Headquarters Marine Corps would no longer arrange officer transfers to ensure contact relief in the training command. Greene protested to Pate, without success, that these new policies could lead to decreased supervision of recruit training.[32]

The Headquarters Marine Corps staff did come up with one answer to Greene's officer assignment complaints. In a letter on March 7, 1957, Pate directed Greene to institute the "series" system successfully used by San Diego for over a year. This system involved forming four platoons at a time in the same company and battalion. The four would go through the entire training schedule together under the supervision of a series officer, usually a first lieutenant, and a series gunnery sergeant. Pate said this system provided the needed officer supervision with greater economy of personnel. This economy included maintaining only three training battalions rather than the four then in operation at Parris Island. Further, the direct supervision of the series officer eliminated the requirement that all platoons of a company be billeted in one area. Finally, Pate's letter, which was drafted by the G–3 division at

Headquarters, directed Greene to submit a recommended table of organization to support the series system. These recommendations were to be at Headquarters by the first of April.[33]

In the nine months after the creation of the Recruit Training Command, Pate and the Headquarters staff had completely shifted their policies toward the training command. In May 1956 Brigadier General Greene had a free hand and could get anyone and anything he desired. However, as the monetary and personnel costs mounted, and the Ribbon Creek incident became a memory, other priorities occupied the attention of Headquarters and the Commandant. For example, in December 1956 Greene had requested substantial personnel increases without success. Pate had replied that such increases could not be granted without detriment to the operating forces.[34] In essence, the Recruit Training Command, shorn of Shoup's bulldozer advocacy, became just another voice among the many competing for the attention of the Headquarters staff.

Wallace Greene, aware that maltreatment of recruits at Parris Island had declined rather than disappeared, still considered the dangers to the Marine Corps as serious as in the immediate aftermath of Ribbon Creek. His responsibilities remained just as great. However, his access to resources had diminished, and he had become increasingly isolated from the centers of power in the Headquarters staff. His frustrations increased, but he was not about to give up yet.

7

Greene's Downfall

Late in 1956, as the automatic, crisis-level type of support from Headquarters Marine Corps waned, Brigadier General Greene became increasingly frustrated with the failure of Headquarters to provide him with the quality of public relations support he desired. From the beginning he had not been satisfied with the system for handling public affairs at the recruit depot. The officer responsible for these duties had no professional training in the field, and Headquarters refused to send a fully qualified man to fill the position. In addition, the commandant's instructions establishing the Recruit Training Command assigned public relations to the depot headquarters, not the training command. This arrangement left the depot public affairs office neither as well staffed nor as responsive as General Greene desired.[1]

The situation worried Wallace Greene. He knew the pervasiveness of the training abuses existing before the Ribbon Creek incident, and he was aware that some drill instructors surreptitiously continued their maltreatment of recruits. Should this lead to another major incident, he reasoned, the Marine Corps could lose its public support, not to mention the dangers inherent in a full-scale congressional investigation. Something had to be done.[2]

John R. Blandford, the senior staff member of the House Armed Services Committee, who was also a Marine Corps Reserve lieutenant colonel, suggested a solution to Greene's public affairs apprehensions. Blandford spent his two weeks of annual reserve duty during September 1956 working for Major General Shoup in Washington. Blandford provided the Marine Corps with a list of questions he believed would be raised in any congressional investigation of Marine recruit training, plus his own recommendations for precluding such an investigation.

Among his recommendations was one calling for trained public affairs officers at the two recruit depots. Another suggested the depots initiate a program of four-to-five-day visits to the depots by small groups of civic leaders. Blandford said such visits could best be done over several months to prevent the image of staged performances. While at the depot, the groups should be given full freedom to go anywhere and see everything.[3]

Pate circulated Blandford's recommendations to the recruit depots and the Headquarters staff. Greene and Brigadier General Alan Shapley, who headed the Recruit Training Command at San Diego, California, endorsed both these proposals.

The personnel section at Headquarters supported neither proposal. The section's position was that visits by recruits' families would be better than ones by a few community leaders. Further, the personnel section noted that the assignment of additional public affairs experts to the two depots could occur only at the expense of the Fleet Marine Force, the Corps' combat arm. The latter position differed from an earlier willingness to give the training commands to everyone for whom they asked. However, it conformed to the Commandant's policy of enhancing the readiness of Marine combat forces.[4]

Greene recognized that Blandford's public relations recommendations were not going to be approved by Headquarters Marine Corps; he would have to act on his own initiative. Greene began organizing visits by community leaders to Parris Island. He obtained the necessary aircraft from the 2d Marine Aircraft Wing at Cherry Point, North Carolina; the various Marine Corps Reserve and Recruitment District commanders provided the contacts with local civic leaders.[5]

These visits were carefully planned and conducted. The groups were no larger than twenty-five people to avoid exceeding the capacity of the available Marine transport planes. En route to Parris Island, each group received biographies of General Greene and Major General Homer L. Litzenberg, the commander of the depot, to acquaint them with the two Marine generals. The visitors also would read copies of one of Greene's speeches covering his training goals and policies. At Parris Island, the visitors followed standardized tours of the training facilities with some of the more rugged events, such as pugil-stick fights, presented by instructors rather than recruits.[6]

These VIP visits were a big success. The delegation from the South Carolina legislature, for example, submitted a resolution, quickly passed by both houses of the General Assembly, expressing their gratitude and favorable impression of Marine training at Parris Island.

Greene's public relations campaign included much more than these organized VIP tours. Local groups, such as the Boy Scouts, received the same treatment. Prominent local individuals enjoyed use of the Parris Island golf course. Parents of recruits could visit their sons and daughters at any time; however, they were encouraged to delay the visit until the latter part of the training cycle or, preferably, graduation day. Further, Parris Island welcomed all visitors, including members of the press. The latter had no difficulty in obtaining interviews with General Greene. By March 1957 over 30,000 visitors had been to the base.[7]

General Greene's public relations program was a good one. It even had the potential of diverting press attention from the continuing string of maltreatment cases brought to court-martial. There was, however, one major obstacle to that goal: Bem Price, the highly respected reporter for the Associated Press, whose bylined articles on Parris Island irritated Wallace Greene.

The disagreement between Greene and Price grew out of the changing nature of military/press relations in the 1950s. A decade earlier, during World War II, there had been a consensus of purpose between the military and the press. They formed a team with the common goal of defeating the nation's enemies and encouraging troop and home-front morale. This remained, by and large, the military's concept of the role of the press. By the end of the Korean War, however, military/press relations were changing. The press moved, depending upon one's point of view, to either a more objective or an antagonistic stance toward the military and the executive branch in general.[8] This situation reached its zenith during Vietnam and Watergate, but was present, if not so apparent, in the mid-1950s.

These two views of the role of the press in American society collided at Parris Island. Assigned to Parris Island to reform Marine recruit training by eradicating maltreatment, Greene needed the press as a vehicle for getting his message to the American public and his fellow Marines. In his situation, it was a tool for reform. Price, on the other hand, as a professional newsman assigned to report on Parris Island, sought to print the truth as he saw it about the continuing problems at the base.

Other reporters, however, managed to report the truth as they saw it without antagonizing Wallace Greene or hindering the accomplishment of his mission. Greene's problem was that Bem Price was not some uninformed reporter who quickly wrote a story based upon a guided, whirlwind tour of Parris Island, a brief interview with General Greene, and public affairs handouts.

Bem Price was a veteran of thirteen years of reserve and active duty service in the Marine Corps. He had served as the public affairs officer of the 1st Marine Division in Korea where he received the Legion of Merit to go with the Bronze Star Medal he earned on Okinawa in World War II.[9]

Bem Price, through personal experience, knew the Marine Corps intimately and, as a member of the Marine Corps "family," had no trouble finding the inevitable skeletons in the family closet. Spending a few hours in the bar of the Staff NCO club always provided good leads. Following these up, he then wrote feature stories that factually reported the situation at Parris Island. His articles made it clear that Greene had not eliminated the long-standing maltreatment problem or the attitudes that encouraged it. Given the resistance by some Marines at Parris Island to Greene's reforms, and the continuing courts-martial for maltreatment, Price automatically complicated Greene's chances of ending training abuses.

The Associated Press continued from time to time to assign Bem Price to report on Parris Island and recruit training. In November 1956 he wrote that assault, maltreatment, and illicit financial dealings were well recognized as the standard problems at Parris Island. Price's story put Greene's fundamental problems on the front pages of America's newspapers, something General Greene wished to avoid.

This news story reflected Bem Price's considerable experience as both a reporter and a Marine public affairs officer. He had not been swayed by the same packaged tour, the same presentations on the new training system as had other newsmen.[10] His articles did not indicate any particular nostalgia for the Marine Corps, which was understandable, since his job was to report the news, not to act as a publicist for the Corps.

Price came back to Parris Island in late February 1957 to cover a series of courts-martial involving drill instructors. In one of the trials the DI defendant was quickly exonerated, and Price could see no reason for holding the trial in the first place, except to forestall possible charges of trying to cover up maltreatment. Price wrote that "the Marines reduced the supposedly grim court-martial almost to the level of farce." He went on to say that drill instructors now had the threat of court-martial always hanging over their heads, and they believed they did not have enough leeway under the new training system.[11]

Following the appearance of this article, the headquarters of the recruit depot, which had the actual responsibility for courts-martial, became less cooperative with Bem Price. The depot chief of staff denied Price's request for special telephone lines adjacent to the court room on the grounds that a pay telephone was only 200 feet away. The depot public affairs office refused to give Price the home addresses of recruits who were expected to appear as witnesses at the trial and denied Price's photographer the use of the depot photographic laboratory.[12]

General Greene took a more drastic step. He wrote General Pate in Washington asking him to get the Associated Press to pull Price out of Parris Island before the next court-martial, which was scheduled during March. Greene told Pate that Price had "twisted . . . news to a degree highly detrimental to the Marine Corps and the public interest." As evidence, he provided Pate with an analysis of fifteen of Price's stories that, in Greene's opinion, indicated a bias against both Corps and Pate. Finally, Greene recommended that, in the event Price was not replaced, he be barred from all Marine Corps installations.[13]

Greene's letter was an unfortunate mistake because, as the trial soon revealed, Bem Price had been correct in his assessment. Depot staff officers, over whom Greene had no control, had botched the pretrial investigations. Specifically, as Greene learned only later, they had pressured recruits into signing statements that could not be sustained in court.[14] The recruits' actual testimony did not match the written statements they had been coerced into signing. This fiasco, though not of Greene's doing, ultimately lowered his standing with Pate.

Price's articles, though a source of frustration to General Greene, were not the latter's only source of outside concern. Since November 1956 there had been an ongoing investigation of a citizens' group that was distributing questionnaires about maltreatment at Parris Island. The group sent the questionnaires to former recruits who had been discharged from the Marine Corps for unsuitability. The most likely source of the addresses of these men was a person who worked at Parris Island itself. The investigation involved not only local military authorities but also the Federal Bureau of Investigation (FBI). There seemed to be reasons for suspecting subversive intent, but, eventually, the FBI reported no Communist involvement in the group's activities. Local authorities eventually arrested the civilian employee at the recruit depot who was suspected of taking the addresses from official files, but quietly hushed up the case because it was rather messy and involved allegations of homosexual activity.[15] However, at the time Greene wrote Pate asking to have Price removed from the base, the investigation was still in progress. Thus, in March 1957, there appeared to be some grounds for General Greene and his staff to suspect subversive activity being directed against the Marine Corps and Parris Island.

Another contemporary case linked subversive activities with the press at the national level. There had been a series of hearings by the Senate Internal Security Subcommittee during which several witnesses refused to provide the names of persons they knew to be Communists. One of those who refused to testify was a newsman who had been convicted of the charge of refusing to testify shortly before Greene wrote to Pate about Bem Price.[16] Again, in hindsight, there was no connection to Parris Island or Bem Price. However, given the prevalent national paranoia over subversion and "monolithic" Communism in the 1950s, the picture was less than clear when Greene wrote Pate on March 8, 1957.

That March, Wallace Greene considered the three elements—Price's articles, the questionnaires, and the trial of the newsman—to be part of a larger picture. Because of the apparent connection and a genuine personal concern over the problem, General Greene signed and distributed a letter drafted by his chief of staff. The letter, bearing a "Confidential" security classification, went to all Marine general officers heading major east coast commands.

The letter claimed that subversive elements sought to exploit every incident that indicated brutality existed at Parris Island. Subversives allegedly were trying to show that Marine authorities knew of such practices and covered them up. In addition, according to the letter, these elements were attempting to drive a wedge between Marine officers and noncommissioned officers by slanting the news to show drill instructors as victims of a system in which officers demanded harsh treatment of recruits, but awarded courts-martial to those caught doing so. If this subversive campaign succeeded, the letter said, public opinion might force the Department of Defense to step in and "standardize" Marine recruit training along the lines of the other services.[17] The unstated message was that such standardization might destroy the Marine Corps as an elite fighting force, thus weakening the national defense.

The following day, March 9, 1957, Bem Price dropped another bombshell. He published a report by a depot staff officer, which alleged widespread disobedience by drill instructors of the regulations prohibiting maltreatment of recruits. Greene was furious and immediately wrote General Pate to deny the charge. "The only truth [in the report]," he wrote, ". . . is this—that a large percentage of DIs do not believe that thumping is bad or that it is not a good way to train a recruit."* He emphasized, however, that the great majority of the DIs obeyed the regulations because they were good Marines.[18]

Later that day the depot public affairs office made two separate press releases. The first contained a copy of a letter from Greene to the Charleston, South Carolina *News and Courier*. The letter sought to establish the "non-factual basis" of Price's latest article, and to counter any negative effects it might have had on "the morale, loyalty, efficiency, and discipline" of Parris Island's drill instructors.[19] The second release, which did not go out until 9:00 o'clock that night, said:

> General Wallace M. Greene, Jr., commanding Parris Island's Recruit Training Command, announced tonight that he was certain that subversive elements were using publicity concerning maltreatment cases to further their own causes by attempting to destroy public trust and confidence in the Marine Corps and to undermine morale, discipline, and the efficiency of the Nation's combat ready forces.
>
> General Greene said that his staff had just completed a detailed study of this subject.
>
> In view of the present Senate hearings on this matter, General Greene has forwarded his opinions to higher headquarters for consideration.[20]

In neither release did General Greene call Bem Price a subversive or a Communist. However, William L. Beale, Jr., the Associated Press bureau chief in Washington, believed that, when combined, the two news releases, with their similar wording, implied a subver-

---

* "Thumping" was a common boot-camp slang word for the hitting of a recruit. One apocryphal practice by DIs to correct wayward recruits in the evening was known (perhaps based upon the old method of controlling a day's routine with bugle calls) as "thump call."

sive intent behind Price's feature articles. He immediately decided to fight that implication. He telephoned Bem Price, who was already asleep at his home in McLean, Virginia. Beale told him to come to the office, where they began drafting a summary of the events in the case. The next morning Beale asked the Secretary of the Navy for an appointment.[21]

General Pate returned to Washington from a visit to North Carolina on March 12 and quickly wrote a personal letter to General Greene. Pate said everyone at Headquarters was "in a dither" over the press releases. "For heaven's sake," he added, "say nothing again that will alienate the press."[22]

The next day Pate learned that Mr. Beale would be meeting with the Secretary of the Navy the following morning. The AP was clearly determined to repudiate the implications it saw in Greene's statement. General Pate met with the Secretary after the AP interview, and then telephoned the bureau chief to smooth over the incident. Pate also invited Bem Price to lunch that same day. The luncheon proved amicable, and Price was willing to let the matter drop.[23]

The Commandant did not forgive Greene as easily as did Bem Price. On March 20 he received a letter of explanation in which Greene said the news release on subversives was done in the Marine Corps' best interests. "This is not the case," replied Pate. "It has put me in a very embarrassing position and I am having trouble wiggling out of it."[24] The Commandant was referring to interest in the allegations expressed by the Senate Internal Security Subcommittee, which, eventually, Pate managed to deflect.

Pate's letter to Greene went on to say that he was changing his plans regarding the assignments of general officers during the coming year. Greene was to leave Parris Island in July to assume command of Camp Lejeune, North Carolina. Pate explained it was time for a change at Parris Island because Greene had been under a tremendous strain recently. Further, he ordered Greene to stay away from the drill instructors during his remaining time at Parris Island.[25]

Despite the polite language, General Pate actually was saying that he was relieving Greene from command for cause. The implication of unsatisfactory performance makes the phrase "relieved for cause" one of the most dreaded in a professional officer's career. The letter also virtually confined Greene to his office during his remaining time at Parris Island.

Leaving Headquarters Marine Corps at about the same time as Pate's devastating letter was Greene's fitness report for the period ending February 28, 1957, and ostensibly signed on March 1, 1957, by Pate, who was Greene's reporting senior. Pate did not mention this fitness report in his letter of March 20. The report gave Greene "outstanding" marks in all categories except for an "excellent" for administrative duties. Two categories were marked "not observed." The first of these was "endurance," the other was "presence of mind," the latter a combat-related category covering the "ability to think and act promptly and effectively in an unexpected emergency or under great strain."[26] A "not observed" mark for presence of mind was normal in peacetime.

This fitness report was, at best, a marginal one for a general officer. For that reason, the forwarding letter, signed by a staff officer at Headquarters, asked Greene to complete Section F and return the report to Washington. Section F provided space for an officer to rebut an unsatisfactory fitness report. Greene merely checked the block indicating he did not desire to make a statement, and returned the report on March 24, 1957.

This is not to say that General Greene accepted the report calmly. His first reaction had been to fight back. He drafted an angry message to the Commandant demanding a court of inquiry to determine the facts concerning the wide extent of maltreatment at Parris Island prior to his arrival there. Further, he requested he not be transferred until completion of the investigation.[27]

Wallace Green did not send the message. To have done so might have exposed to the world the extent of abuses at Parris Island prior to Ribbon Creek, and risked destroying all that Greene had accomplished at Parris Island. Instead of sending the message, General Greene cooled down, filed the draft away, and then wrote a long, more reasoned letter to General Pate giving his side of the Bem Price controversy. He even challenged the assertion that he had been under great strain in recent months. He stated that just the opposite was the case; a recent physical examination at the naval hospital had shown him to be in the best of health.[28] This letter, however, did not change Pate's mind about transferring General Greene.

The remainder of Greene's stay at Parris Island was relatively quiet. Bem Price was elsewhere, the press seemed to have backed off, and there were no major controversies about Marine training. On May 23, 1957, there was a farewell party for General and Mrs. Greene at the officers club. The following morning they left Parris

Island in the family car. A military police car provided an escort. At the main gate the Greenes passed through a double line of saluting Marines and massed national and Marine Corps colors.[29]

Anyone with a knowledge of the American military services could have guessed the effect of this peremptory reassignment on Wallace Greene's career. A safe bet was that it was at a dead end. He was, in fact, passed over for promotion to major general by the next selection board.

In the months prior to his transfer from Parris Island, Brigadier General Greene won his public relations battles on the local and regional levels, but lost it at the national level because of Price's accurate reports in the press. In addition, Greene's unfortunate charge of Communist subversive activities directed toward Parris Island damaged a bright career.

That analysis does not go far enough. An additional conclusion is that Wallace Greene risked his career to protect the Marine Corps from an apparent subversive campaign. His action—whether considered a sacrifice or simply an error in judgment—may have helped avert a congressional investigation of continuing abuses at Parris Island. In any event, both the Marine Corps and the press moved in a way that cooled the situation. Pate transferred Greene to North Carolina, and the Associated Press gave Bem Price assignments elsewhere.

Thereafter the press in general paid less attention to Parris Island. Admittedly, there were cases of maltreatment reported in the press in subsequent years, but there was no great public outcry—at least until after the Vietnam War. In fact, not until 1976 did public and congressional pressure force further significant changes in Marine recruit training.

There is no evidence that in 1957 either General Greene or Bem Price thought of their disagreement in terms of differing views of the role of the press in American society. Such an on-the-spot analysis might have been possible at Parris Island had there been a skilled, professional press officer—a person with a foot in both camps—assigned to the recruit depot's headquarters. Had that been the case, both sides would have been well served, and Wallace Greene perhaps would not have laid his career on the line.

8

Postscript

The departure of Brigadier General Greene marked the end of the third phase of the Marine Corps' response to the Ribbon Creek incident. The first of these had been the crisis reaction, which lasted until the Corps had created a Recruit Training Command at each recruit depot and revised its training program. The issuing of the new field hats to drill instructors symbolically marked the end of that phase.

The second phase at Parris Island involved two elements, which at times worked against each other. Greene's efforts to complete the permanent institutionalization of his reforms was the key element. The reform movement slowed, however, as Headquarters Marine Corps found it impossible to maintain the surge of men and money going into recruit training at the expense of other sectors of the Marine Corps.

The final phase, which occurred long after Greene's departure, contained the Marine Corps' final resolution of the Ribbon Creek affair. This meant regularizing the training organization by changing the training commands, with their skeleton staffs, into recruit training regiments commanded by a colonel with the assistance of a full staff complement. The regimental commander reported to the depot commander rather than directly to the Commandant of the Marine Corps. This command relationship continues today.

None of the foregoing discussion of phases should obscure the salient point about the Corps' response to Ribbon Creek. Specifically, the limited reforms were in the area of supervision and scarcely affected the nature of the searing experience endured by new recruits. General Greene himself pointed out that the reforms deliberately did not alter the "shock treatment" given recruits upon their entry into training. This training method, long a part of boot camp, meant the rapid, forceful tearing away of the recruit's civilian identity—his hair style, his mode of clothing, unmilitary habits—and remolding him into a Marine. This was the heart of the boot camp experience and, true to his instructions, General Greene preserved it. This may have been his major contribution to the whole affair.[1]

Boot camp has remained the Marine Corps' equivalent of a tribal puberty rite, and this institutional significance has kept the Corps from forgetting the Ribbon Creek affair. In fact, the shock the affair caused the institution probably has more relevance to today's Marines than such traumatic battles as Tarawa or such spectacular victories as the landing at Inchon. The veterans of World War II are long gone from the Corps' ranks; the last Korean War enlisted Marines have completed their thirty years of service and slipped into retirement. Probably only a handful of those who experienced pre-Ribbon Creek recruit training remain on active service. Nevertheless, Ribbon Creek is a fresh lesson for every officer and drill instructor involved in modern recruit training. The Marine Corps still has little tolerance for those whose actions create bad publicity about recruit training methods.

The Corps' 1956 response to Ribbon Creek remains the model it has used in handling all subsequent training incidents. Whenever such incidents occur, the Marines reach back and dust off that model. For example, when training problems provoked congressional hearings in 1976, the Marine Corps again responded with the Ribbon Creek formula: assigning larger numbers of officers, increased officer supervision of training, and tighter psychological screening of prospective DIs. There are, of course, few other options, barring a complete change in recruit training philosophy.[2]

In fairness, one must say that the Marine Corps has taken major steps in that direction. There are now two officers assigned to each series, one of whom is present from reveille in the morning to taps at night. The official approach to training is that it be conducted in a "low-stress" environment. That low stress, however, refers to psychological pressures. Boot camp is still tough, and the physical effort required is demanding. The overall quality of recruit is high, with well over 90 percent possessing high school diplomas. Those who cannot adapt to the Marine Corps are quickly discharged, a policy that benefits the individual, the DIs, and the Marine Corps as a whole. While some old salts may grumble about the current approach, the actual quality of Marine probably exceeds that in the 1930s, that earlier "golden age" of high-quality enlistees.

The Marine Corps, nevertheless, does well to keep the Ribbon Creek tragedy's memory alive. Had the Corps not handled its 1956 response with political skill, a full-scale congressional investigation could have precipitated a staggering institutional crisis. The Marines' cherished recruit training system might not have survived the revelations arising from such an investigation. Even as it was, the furor, including that from pro-Marine lobbies, buffeted the Corps for months.

There were, of course, some who welcomed any threat to an American institution such as the Marine Corps. General Greene believed, and still believes, that much of the adverse publicity after Ribbon Creek was directly inspired by Communist subversives.[3] On reflection, it is logical that any bona-fide Communist would have been ideologically derelict had he or she not had such a goal. It is just as logical to assume that the Communist party would seek to use Ribbon Creek against the Marine Corps.

This is not to say, however, that any such campaign had any meaningful substance or any significant effect upon the American public. Indeed, the primary lasting effect upon the public was a concern for the safety of sons contemplating enlisting in the Corps. Recruiters became adept at calming such fears.

Why, one may rightfully ask, did the Marine Corps wait until it had a tragedy on its hands before it moved to clean up its training system? Certainly, there were enough indications of the problem over the previous six years. The answer is that the Marines did make a quiet, unpublicized, but unsuccessful attempt to eliminate maltreatment in recruit training during the Korean War.

The effort at reform, which began with the assignment of Major General Silverthorn to Parris Island, failed for a number of reasons. The effort simply did not touch upon the fundamental causes of maltreatment. Instead, it emphasized rapid and severe punishment of offenders. Unfortunately, Silverthorn's policies did not have the active and dedicated support of the majority of the commissioned officers at Parris Island. The base had become a professional backwater, a haven for too many officers in the twilight of their careers. Other officers were reservists unhappy with being involuntarily called to active duty for the Korean War. Inevitably, those officers possessing the drive necessary to carry out a reform campaign were far outnumbered by disgruntled reservists and tired old war-horses who didn't want their comfortable sinecure disturbed.

Another reason, probably the primary one, for the failure of Silverthorn's campaign to eradicate maltreatment was that the NCOs, the DIs who actually trained recruits, opposed the reforms. The nub of the opposition was that they perceived "thumping" as being in their corporate best interests. At the time, the NCO corps was itself undergoing an institutional crisis. World War II left the Corps bloated with numbers of NCOs in excess of its actual needs. Further, these men proved "long on combat experience but short on professional maturity and training and leadership skills."[4] These Marines had little hope for advancement, especially after reductions in the Corps caused many temporary officers to revert to their permanent enlisted ranks.

In addition, the NCOs, as well as the entire defense establishment, were having to adapt to a whole new legal system, the Uniform Code of Military Justice, which included checks to traditional NCO authority. The new legal code demanded more sophisticated leadership skills; developing them was a slow, painful, frustrating process. The Marine Corps at the time did not even have any formal schools for its senior and mid-level NCOs, which could have eased the transition.

Marine NCOs perceived their status and prestige slipping away—everywhere *except* at the recruit depots where DIs ruled supreme. *Only* at the recruit depots did NCOs retain their idealized level of authority, *only* there could they shape the nature of the Marine Corps' enlisted ranks by instilling in recruits an awesome respect for NCOs.

These pressures on the corporate ranks of Marine NCOs inevitably affected the way DIs treated their recruits. Peer pressure accentuated the process by condoning and encouraging maltreatment. Further, these institutional pressures pushed the NCOs closer together and united them against officers who might try to alter the training system. They would not even turn against a fellow DI unless he hospitalized a recruit with injuries. Edwin McDowell, in his novel *To Keep Our Honor Clean,* which takes place at Parris Island during the Korean War, has one dialogue in which a senior drill instructor admits he would not turn in a subordinate DI for a maltreatment episode. The reason: he wouldn't do anything to jeopardize the position of an NCO.[5] Similar thinking among real NCOs made Ribbon Creek or some other tragedy inevitable at Parris Island.

The Marine Corps responded to Ribbon Creek with considerable political skill, but made some mistakes in the follow-through on its agreement with Congress. Given the damage-limiting nature of that agreement, and Pate's weaknesses as Commandant, Generals Shoup and Greene were not the best choices for their new assignments. In a damage-limiting scenario, hard-driving achievers need a steady hand upon the reins if they are to remain within the bounds of limited goals. This is not a condemnation of Shoup and Greene, but illustrates Pate's stature as Commandant. Pate lacked the strength and moral courage to smooth away the tensions created by the situation. Greene and Shoup worked hard to bring their perception of their mandate to fruition without sufficient guidance and support from Pate. As it was, Greene began to think of the Headquarters Marine Corps staff as an impediment rather than an ally.

The best choice for Inspector-General for Recruit Training, given Pate's weaknesses, would have been Major General Twining, the man who put together the agreement with Congress. No one else had a better knowledge of the situation; in addition, Twining had the stature, intellectual capacity, and polished political skills to have instituted the needed changes without alienating the Headquarters staff. He possessed the abilities needed to weld the recruit training commands and the Headquarters staff into a functioning team.

General Pate should be viewed not as the villain of this episode but as the weak link. Pate, who was probably already ill, was unable to foresee and prevent problems. In fact, the successes of his tenure as Commandant reflect the quality of his staff officers more than his own. Pate at least had the wisdom to call in competent people when he needed help. He prudently followed recommendations to bring in Twining to manage the Ribbon Creek problem, but erred in allowing Twining to return to the west coast. However, as soon as Twining received his third star as a lieutenant general, Pate brought him back to command the base at Quantico, Virginia, located just south of Washington. This, at least, put Twining close at hand where he could help keep Pate out of trouble.

Twining emerges as the hero of the Corps' battle to preserve the fundamental nature of its recruit training. He was, however, an unsung hero because his efforts took place outside the public eye. He never publicly received the credit he deserved. He would have received that recognition had he remained in Washington as Inspector-General for Recruit Training. Returning to California cost him that chance. On the other hand, this move kept him above the turmoil over Ribbon Creek and improved his chances for promotion to lieutenant general. Once he attained that rank and moved to Quantico, Twining became almost a shadow Commandant as he helped his friend Pate complete his final years as a Marine.

The gritty job of implementing the agreement with Congress fell to Shoup, Greene, and Shapley. The latter's assignment at San Diego, where abuse had always been less prevalent, never attracted the public scrutiny to the extent endured by Parris Island.

Shoup, as Inspector-General for Recruit Training, bulldozed over the Headquarters Marine Corps staff to such an extent that he was kicked upstairs to be Inspector-General of the Marine Corps. This assignment theoretically encompassed his old duties regarding recruit training, but a standing Marine Corps order, MCO 5041.1, entrusted the responsibility for inspecting the conduct of recruit training to the G–3 division of Headquarters Marine Corps. Shoup, as Inspector-General, could only conduct administrative inspections of the depots.

This left General Greene out on a limb at Parris Island. Shorn of his protector, Shoup, Greene could only work through Pate, which proved unsatisfactory.

Greene began his limited reforms at Parris Island with the full support of the depot's NCOs. That support subsequently declined, as indicated by an increase in the number of courts-martial in the summer of 1956. This loss of support occurred despite Greene's habitual daily inspections of the training and his face-to-face discussions with DIs, which communicated his wishes, training philosophy, and the force of his personality.

Working against him were several negative factors. The assignment of significantly larger numbers of students to DI school appeared, to the working DIs at least, as preparation for a mass relief of DIs. Next, too many DIs came to view the newly assigned cadre of officers as spies, "sneaky petes" or hatchet men ready to pounce upon any DI for the slightest infraction of training rules. Punishment for infractions were swift and, to the dismay of many NCOs and their families, often far heavier than Staff Sergeant McKeon received for a much more serious offense. Furthermore, the DIs' promotions, careers, and family income depended upon receiving high marks on their periodic fitness reports. This made top-quality platoons vital to promotion chances because officers usually assigned fitness-report markings based upon results of the competition among the four platoons in a series. This placed tremendous pressure upon all DIs, regardless of their leadership skills. For some NCOs, physical intimidation was the easiest way out.

The level of maltreatment, nevertheless, did decline significantly under Greene's stewardship, partly because of the DIs' new perquisites, the vigilance of the officers, and the positive feedback from various major commands extolling the improved quality of recruit graduates.

Greene's success in reducing maltreatment did not create a self-perpetuating process that could be left alone. It worked only so long as Greene—and his successors—made their desires felt throughout the depot's training establishment. General Greene himself took not a single day off from his duties at Parris Island. He recognized how easily things could unravel.

Headquarters Marine Corps was aware of this reality. As a consequence, the command of the Recruit Training Regiment; the successor of the Recruit Training Command, became a high-visibility position for top-quality colonels likely to become general officers.

General Greene's most intractable problem at Parris Island, and the cause of his relief from command, stemmed from the growing mutual distrust between the military and the press. During Greene's tenure at the training command, the major press figure was Bem Price, one of the Associated Press's senior reporters. The misunderstandings spiraled upward. The command never managed to give Price an appreciation of the philosophical base and goals for the changes at the depot. Price, wary of the official press releases, sought additional information from the DIs, the very group that felt most threatened by the changes in the training system. As a result, despite Price's professional efforts to achieve balance, his stories gave emphasis to the DIs perspective, and they could be critical of the command. Bem Price's feature stories, which appeared in over 90 percent of the nation's newspapers, cost Greene needed support among the staff of Headquarters Marine Corps and General Pate, not to mention the DIs themselves. Price's accounts of dissatisfaction created new dissatisfaction, and a self-perpetuating spiral. Greene's two news releases, which appeared to equate negative news stories with subversive activities, proved the final straw, and General Pate relieved him of his duties.

Greene's suspicions of a Communist conspiracy did not precipitate this relief, since Pate himself took the idea seriously enough quietly to refer the matter to J. Edgar Hoover, the head of the FBI. Apparently after consulting with his staff, Hoover discounted the threat; but even had it existed, Greene's news releases would have got him into hot water with the Headquarters bureaucracy. Greene's error in this respect was in making his releases without prior clearance from his superiors. In doing so, Greene, a very junior brigadier, went outside proper channels and, in essence, took upon himself the jealously guarded prerogatives of his seniors. In any bureaucracy, military or otherwise, such assumptions of power can be fatal, as Greene's relief proved.

The other side of the coin was that Greene's two news releases actually did affect the course of press coverage of Parris Island. The Associated Press backed away from the recruit training scene as a continuing news event and sent Bem Price to cover other stories. No other segment of the national press took up the recruit training story and Parris Island moved further from the front pages of the nation's newspapers. Greene, in this respect, inadvertently had succeeded in cooling the situation.

Neither Wallace Greene nor any other Marine commander has eradicated maltreatment of recruits. The problem is endemic, and keeping it within acceptable levels represents the best anyone has accomplished. "We seem never to be able to get out of this problem, particularly at Parris Island," said Lieutenant General John R. Chaisson in a 1972 speech, "because, I would say, or use the term 'too frequently,' something happens down there, either a fatality or something of that nature."[6]

The problem will remain as long as recruit training serves as the primary method of socialization for enlisted Marines. It provides the one common experience that creates solidarity and group identification as "Marines," whether they be infantrymen, artillerymen, warehousemen, or computer programmers.

The Ribbon Creek affair, besides leaving a lasting impression on recruit training, also affected the lives and careers of the drama's principal players. It placed General Pate and his term as Commandant under a cloud that never dissipated. Many enlisted Marines and some officers—who viewed the affair only in terms of their own narrow Marine Corps world—never believed Pate's assertion that the incident had placed the whole Marine Corps on trial. Such men also had difficulty believing the repeated statements by Greene and others that the goal of the training changes was to preserve traditional Marine recruit training, not to destroy it.

Pate's unpopularity increased as Marines began to realize that he was insensitive to their concerns. An example of his lack of propriety occurred during an official inspection trip to units in the Far East. During the trip, Pate stated publicly that the Marine Corps would continue its policy of prohibiting families from accompanying or visiting Marines assigned to those units. Pate had his own wife with him on the trip.[7]

General Pate retired from the Marine Corps on December 31, 1959. He and his wife settled in Beaufort, South Carolina, where he entered into a business relationship with a local real estate company. The latter used Pate's name in advertisements in various service journals inviting officers planning a move to Beaufort to allow General Pate to help them find a home.[8]

Pate's health declined rapidly. Just over a year after his retirement, medical tests revealed a malignant intestinal tumor. He died in Bethesda Naval Hospital in July 1961, and was buried in Arlington National Cemetery with full military honors on August 31.

His story was not finished. His will gave his home in Beaufort to his old school, the Virginia Military Institute. While the terms of the will specified that Mrs. Pate would be permitted to live there for the rest of her life, it did deprive her of the home's financial value. Complicating the problem was the reality that, because of the way the law read at that time, General Pate's retired pay stopped upon his death. Mrs. Pate was left in poor financial straits.[*]

Senior Marines in the Beaufort area notified Headquarters Marine Corps of the situation. The chief of staff of Headquarters asked the Navy medical department to review Pate's records. The review, which concentrated on the physical examination made just prior to Pate's retirement, turned up X-ray evidence of a brain tumor. Based on that, Mrs. Pate qualified for a pension from the Veterans Administration.[9]

Another major character in the Ribbon Creek story, Major General Joseph Burger, also never fully escaped its taint. Of course, his old friend General Pate ensured that Burger received his third star. Burger retired as a lieutenant general in 1961; however, even as late as 1969, when recording an oral history interview for the Marine Corps, Burger remained defensive about the subject of Parris Island.

---

[*] The current law contains provisions for retired military personnel to take a reduced annuity in a program that allows the surviving spouse to continue receiving a portion of the retired pay.

Matthew C. McKeon left Parris Island as a private, but he had a chance to rebuild a career as a Marine. He earned a promotion to corporal in 1958; however, he received a medical discharge in 1959 for a ruptured spinal disk. McKeon and his family settled in West Boylston, Massachusetts, where he became a state inspector of weights and standards. Interviewed by *Newsweek* in 1970, he said he bore no grudges for his conviction because he believed he received what he deserved. He retained a strong sense of remorse for the six "boys" who drowned in Ribbon Creek in April 1956. He told the reporter, "I just keep thinking those guys would be grown men now, with families of their own. You can never forget that."[10]

Emile Zola Berman returned to New York and his thriving law practice, where he continued his specialty in negligence cases. He defended other controversial criminal cases from time to time, including a young black accused of rape in Louisiana in 1964.

Berman's most famous defense, however, was of Sirhan Sirhan, the Arab youth who killed Senator Robert F. Kennedy after the latter expressed support for Israel. Again, Berman served without pay. When asked how he, a Jew, could defend Sirhan, Berman replied, "I'm not defending his crime, only his rights. . . . Sirhan is a symbol of every man's right to a fair trial and this right needs constant reinforcement by people qualified to do it."[11] Emile Zola Berman died in 1981.

Wallace Greene left Parris Island with a shattered career. A selection board in Washington passed over Greene when choosing the next year's batch of major generals. However, his allies among the Corps' top leaders launched a campaign in his behalf and the following selection board recommended his promotion. He pinned on his second star in August 1959. However, since Greene was not a member of Pate's "team," his future prospects were doubtful.

Suddenly, *everything* changed. In choosing a new Commandant in 1959, President Eisenhower reached down past every lieutenant general in the Marine Corps to pick David M. Shoup, a relatively junior major general, to be Pate's successor. A mass retirement of lieutenant and major generals quickly followed.*

---

* One factor affecting these retirements was the expiration on November 1, 1959, of the law providing for "tombstone promotions" of officers of the naval services who had earned personal decorations for combat performance.

Wallace M. Greene, Jr., became a lieutenant general and Shoup's assistant and chief of staff on January 1, 1960.* Four years later he succeeded Shoup as Commandant of the Marine Corps.

The tidal stream known as Ribbon Creek has been largely forgotten by the American public, but the effects of the 1956 tragedy in its waters still shapes the training of Marine recruits. Senior Marines remember the incident with the realization that maltreatment remains a problem and that other tragedies are within the realm of possibility. Lieutenant General John R. Chaisson, then the chief of staff of Headquarters Marine Corps, expressed these enduring concerns in 1972 when he said, "I think there is enough smoke coming out of that place [Parris Island] where there is always going to be a suspicion that there's fire there."[12]

That whiff of smoke remains over Parris Island; however, the same thing cannot be said of Ribbon Creek. There have been no other night marches in its tidal waters. "Tradition," wrote Brigadier General William B. McKean, "will keep Ribbon Creek safe as long as there is Parris Island."[13]

---

* It was, of course, Lieutenant General Greene who requested the reexamination of Pate's medical records, an action that resulted in Mrs. Pate's receiving a Veterans Administration pension.

Notes

INTRODUCTION

1. Capt. Robert C. Meeker, "Fit to Fight," ms. submitted to *Marine Corps Gazette,* Jan. 10, 1957, copy in Greene Papers, Box 43, Folder 10 (Personal Papers Collection, Marine Corps Historical Center, Washington, D.C.), hereafter GP plus box and folder numbers (e.g., GP–43–10); Capt . Frederick S. Thomas, "New Approaches to Recruit Training," *U.S. Naval Institute Proceedings* 83 (October 1957), p. 1045; Brig. Gen. William B. McKean, *Ribbon Creek* (New York: Dial Press, 1958), p. 38, hereafter McKean, *Ribbon Creek.*

2. Morris Janowitz and Roger W. Little, *Sociology and the Military Establishment* (Beverly Hills: Sage Publications, 1974), pp. 78–79; hereafter Janowitz, *Sociology;* Gary B. Nash, *Red, White, and Black: The Peoples of Early America* (Englewood Cliffs, N.J.: Prentice-Hall, 1974), p. 190; Henry Allen, "The Corps," *Washington Post,* Mar. 5, 1972.

3. Drew Middleton, "Rallying the Marines," *New York Times Magazine,* Dec. 4, 1983.

4. Commanding General (CG), Recruit Training Command, Parris Island, letter to Inspector-General for Recruit Training, Sept. 6, 1956, GP–465–2.

5. Morris Janowitz, "Changing Patterns of Organizational Authority: The Military Establishment," *Administrative Science Quarterly,* March 1959, pp. 474–93, reprinted in Morris Janowitz, *Military Conflict: Essays in the Institutional Analysis of War and Peace* (Beverly Hills: Sage Publications, 1975), pp. 228–30, hereafter Janowitz, *Military Conflict;* Samuel A. Stouffer, et al., *The American Soldier: Adjustment during Army Life,* vol. 1 (Princeton: Princeton University Press, 1949), pp. 411–12; McKean, *Ribbon Creek,* p. 39; J. Robert Moskin, *The U.S. Marine Corps Story* (New York: McGraw-Hill, 1977), p. 823.

6. John Greenway, *The Inevitable Americans* (New York: Alfred A. Knopf, 1964), pp. 73–76.

7. Peter Farb, *Man's Rise to Civilization* (New York: Avon, 1973), pp. 98–100.

8. S. L. A. Marshall, *Men against Fire: The Problem of Command in Future War,* reprint ed. (Gloucester: Peter Smith, 1978), pp. 114, 151–52, hereafter Marshall, *Men against Fire;* Janowitz, *Military Conflict,* p. 230; Janowitz, *Sociology,* p. 81.

9. James Finan, "The Making of a Leatherneck," *American Mercury,* April 1951, p. 460.

10. Samuel A. Stouffer, et al., *The American Soldier: Combat and Its Aftermath,* vol. 2 (Princeton: Princeton University Press, 1949), p. 278; Marshall, *Men against Fire,* pp. 151–53; see also Janowitz, *Sociology,* pp. 108–9.

11. David R. Segal, "Leadership and Management: Organization and Theory," in James A. Buck and Lawrence J. Korb, eds., *Military Leadership* (Beverly Hills: Sage Publications, 1980), p. 146.

12. Edwin McDowell, *To Keep Our Honor Clean* (New York: Vanguard Press, 1980), p. 146.

13. "Report on Recruit Training Survey," issued by Headquarters Marine Corps, Washington, D.C., July 1956. Copy in GP–42–6.

CHAPTER 1

1. Elmore A. Champie, *A Brief History of the Marine Corps Recruit Depot, Parris Island, South Carolina, 1891–1962* (Washington, D.C.: Headquarters, U.S. Marine Corps, 1962), p. 3, hereafter Champie, *Parris Island.*

2. Jesse C. Maris, *Remembering* (Privately printed, 1951), p. 26.

3. Ibid., p. 27.

4. John W. Thomason, Jr., "Hate," In *And a Few Marines* (New York: Scribners, 1943), pp. 463–64.

5. Ibid.

6. Don V. Paradis, Oral History Transcript, 1973 (Oral History Collection, Marine Corps Historical Center, Washington, D.C.).

7. Bem Price, " 'Book' Is Sad Story to Marine Noncoms," *Washington Post,* May 27, 1956.

8. Brig. Gen. Samuel R. Shaw, Oral History Transcript, 1970 (Oral History Collection, Marine Corps Historical Center, Washington, D.C.), hereafter Shaw interview.

9. Ibid.

10. Maj. Robert A. Smith, "First to Fight," *Marine Corps Gazette,* November 1976, p. 47, hereafter Smith, "First to Fight."

11. Lt. Gen. Wallace M. Greene, Jr., letter to Col. Robert D. Heinl, Jr., Nov. 19, 1960, Greene Papers, Box 43, Folder 8 (Personal Papers Collection, Marine Corps Historical Center, Washington, D.C.); hereafter GP–box–folder, e.g., GP–43–8.

12. Smith, "First to Fight," p. 44.

13. Capt. Frederick S. Thomas, "New Approaches to Recruit Training," *U.S. Naval Institute Proceedings* 83 (October 1957), pp. 1057–58; hereafter Thomas, "New Approaches."

14. Col. Merrill F. McLane, letter to the editor, *Washington Post,* Dec. 2, 1980.

15. Smith, "First to Fight," p. 44.

16. Ibid.

17. Ibid.

18. Col. Mitchell Paige, *A Marine Named Mitch* (New York: Vantage Press, 1975), p. 15, hereafter Paige, *Mitch.*

19. Ibid., pp. 14–15.

20. Smith, "First to Fight," pp. 49–50.

21. Harry Polete, "Never the Twain . . . ," *Leatherneck,* August 1948, p. 11.

22. Champie, *Parris Island,* p. 10; Bem Price, "McKeon Court-Martial Stirs 'Spit-and-Polish' Marine Post," *Columbus Dispatch,* July 22, 1956, hereafter Price, "McKeon Court-Martial."

23. Price, "McKeon Court-Martial"; Jeremiah O'Leary, "At Parris Island: The Summers of '42 and '72," *Washington Post,* June 25, 1972; hereafter O'Leary, "Parris Island."

24. William Manchester, *Goodbye Darkness: A Memoir of the Pacific War* (Boston: Little, Brown, & Company, 1980), p. 120, hereafter Manchester, *Goodbye Darkness.*

25. Lt. Gen. Wallace M. Greene, Jr., letter to Col. Robert D. Heinl, Jr., Nov. 19, 1960, GP–43–8.

26. O'Leary, "Parris Island."

27. Manchester, *Goodbye Darkness,* pp. 127, 393; Lt. Gen. Robert H. Barrow, testimony, *Hearings on Marine Corps Recruit Training and Recruiting Programs,* House Armed Services Committee (Washington, D.C.: Government Printing Offrice, 1976), pp. 211–12; O'Leary, "Parris Island."

28. O'Leary, "Parris Island."

29. Ralph Turtinan' "Marines Change Tactics, Not Goals," *Minneapolis Star,* Sept. 18, 1956.

30. James Finan, "The Making of a Leatherneck," *American Mercury,* April 1951, p. 453, hereafter Finan, "Making a Leatherneck."

31. Champie, *Parris Island,* p. 15.

32. Ibid., p. 14.

33. Maj. Gen. Merwin H. Silverthorn, memo to Maj. Gen. W. W. Wensinger, May 27, 1952, copy in GP–42–3; Maj. Paul K. Van Riper, Maj. Michael W. Wydo, and Maj. Donald P. Brown, *An Analysis of Marine Corps Training* (Newport: The Naval War College Center for Advanced Research, 1978), p. 256, hereafter Van Riper, *Marine Corps Training.*

34. Tom Bartlett, "Conversations with a Brew," *Leatherneck,*

August 1972, pp. 16–23; Finan, "Making a Leatherneck," p. 455.

35. Thomas, "New Approaches," p. 1058.

36. Adm. Thomas C. Kinkaid, letter to Brig. Gen. William B. McKean, in McKean, *Ribbon Creek* (New York: Dial Press, 1958), p. 260, hereafter McKean, *Ribbon Creek.*

37. Recruit Training Survey, Headquarter Marine Corps, 1956, copy in GP–42–6.

38. Ibid.

39. Depot Inspector to Depot Chief of Staff, Marine Corps Recruit Depot, Parris Island, S.C., Apr. 5, 1957, copy in GP–42–4.

40. McKean, *Ribbon Creek,* p. 194; Bartlett, "Conversations with a Brew," p. 16; Mel Jones, "A Look at MC Boot Camp Today: New Devotion to Some Old Ways," *Navy Times,* May 31, 1976.

41. Mark Kauffman, "How to Make Marines," *Life,* Oct. 5, 1951, pp. 141–49, hereafter Kauffman, "How to Make Marines."

42. "Marine Corps Puts the Blame," *Washington Star,* May 16, 1956.

43. McKean, *Ribbon Creek,* p. 33.

44. Ibid., p. 32.

45. Ibid., p. 33.

46. McKean, *Ribbon Creek,* p. 33; "Record of Courts-Martial, 1950–57." Note, copy in GP–42–3.

47. Maj. Gen. Merwin H. Silverthorn, memo to Commandant of the Marine Corps, June 13, 1952; "Record of Courts-Martial, 1950–57." Both in GP–42–3.

48. Maj. Gen. Merwin H] Silverthorn, memo to Maj. Gen. W. W. Wensinger, May 27, 1952, GP–42–3.

49. Champie, *Parris Island,* p. 14.

50. Ibid., p. 16.

51. Ibid.

52. Van Riper, *Marine Corps Training,* p. 256.

53. Shaw transcript, p. 299.

54. McKean, *Ribbon Creek,* p. 38.

55. Lt. Gen. Joseph C. Burger, Oral History Transcript, 1969 (Oral History Collection, Marine Corps Historical Center, Washington, D.C.), p. 298, hereafter Burger transcript; Shaw transcript, p. 299; McKean, *Ribbon Creek,* p. 25.

56. Anthony Leviero, "Marine Noncoms Caught in Middle," *New York Times,* Apr. 15, 1956; M. Sgt. Paul Sarokin, "Parris Island," *Leatherneck,* September 1956, p. 21.

57. McKean, *Ribbon Creek,* p. 38.

58. Ibid.

59. Ibid.

60. Gen. Wallace M. Greene, Jr., interview, Aug. 31, 1983.

61. Burger transcript, pp. 287–89.
62. Ibid.
63. Kauffman, "How to Make Marines," p. 149.
64. McKean, *Ribbon Creek,* pp. 26, 39, 62.
65. Lt. Gen. Robert H. Barrow, testimony, *Hearings on Marine Corps Recruit Training and Recruiting Programs,* House Armed Services Committee (Washington, D.C.: Government Printing Offrice, 1976), pp. 212–13.
66. Allan R. Millett, *Semper Fidelis: The History of the United States Marine Corps* (New York: Macmillan, 1980), p. 468, hereafter Millett, *Semper Fidelis.*
67. Maj. Robert I. Edwards, interview, Mar. 19, 1981.
68. Burger transcript, p. 300.
69. Special Correspondent, "Six Marine Drill Instructors Convicted of Maltreatment," *Charlotte News and Courier,* Apr. 14, 1956.
70. Gen. Wallace M. Greene, Jr., interview, Aug. 31, 1983.
71. Lt.. Gen. Wallace M. Greene, Jr., letter to Col. Robert D. Heinl, Jr., Nov. 19, 1960, copy in GP–43–8.
72. Millett, *Semper Fidelis,* p. 528; Bem Price, interview, Jan. 17, 1983.
73. McKean, *Ribbon Creek,* p. 503; Burger transcript, p. 287.
74. Lt. Gen. Wallace M. Greene, Jr., letter to Col. Robert D. Heinl, Jr., Nov. 19, 1960, copy in GP–43–8.

CHAPTER 2

1. Brig. Gen. William B. McKean, *Ribbon Creek* (New York: Dial Press, 1958), p. 176, hereafter McKean, *Ribbon Creek.*
2. Ibid., p. 176.
3. Lt. Gen. Joseph C. Burger, Oral History Transcript, 1969 (Oral History Collection, Marine Corps Historical Center, Washington, D.C.), pp. 228–89, hereafter Burger transcript.
4. McKean, *Ribbon Creek,* pp. 53–55.
5. Record of Proceedings, Court of Inquiry, Marine Corps Recruit Depot, Parris Island, S.C., with endorsements, dated Apr. 20, 1956 (Reference Files, Marine Corps Historical Center, Washington, D.C.), hereafter Inquiry Report.
6. McKean, *Ribbon Creek,* pp. 53, 60.
7. Ibid., p. 64.
8. George MacGillivray, "Historic Guadalcanal Maps in Collection," *Fortitudine* (Spring–Summer 1982), p. 12.
9. McKean, *Ribbon Creek,* p. 412.
10. Inquiry Report, p. 8.
11. Ibid.

12. Albion C. Hailey, "Marines Fear Ease-Up in Boot Training," *Washington Post,* Apr. 15, 1956, hereafter Hailey, "Marines Fear Ease-Up."

13. Inquiry Report, p. 8.

14. Ibid.

15. Hailey, "Marines Fear Ease-Up."

16. Inquiry Report, p. 8.

17. Ibid., p. 9.

18. Ibid.

19. Pvt. Richard B. Brown, court-martial testimony, quoted in McKean, *Ribbon Creek,* p. 152.

20. Inquiry Report, p. 9.

21. Associated Press, "Marine Court Hears Details of Tragedy," *Washington Post,* Apr. 12, 1956; S. Sgt. Matthew C. McKeon, court-martial testimony, quoted in McKean, *Ribbon Creek,* pp. 433–34.

22. Clay Blair, Jr., "The Tragedy of Platoon 71 Puts Marine Training under Fire," *Life* (Apr. 23, 1956), pp. 52–54.

23. "Boystown Marine Related Experience in Death March," Arlington, N.J., *Observer,* May 17, 1956, copy in Greene Papers (Personal Papers Collection, Marine Corps Historical Center, Washington, D.C.), Box 42, Folder 12, hereafter GP–box number–folder number (e.g., GP–42–12).

24. McKean, *Ribbon Creek,* p. 9.

25. Ibid., p. 9–10.

26. Ibid., p. 14.

27. Burger transcript, p. 290.

28. McKean, *Ribbon Creek,* p. 23.

29. Bem Price (former AP senior reporter), interview by author, Jan. 17, 1983, hereafter Price interview.

30. "Marine Court of Inquiry Conducting Daily Secret Hearings on Sunday's Death March," *Beaufort Gazette,* Apr. 12, 1956, copy in GP–43–2.

31. Burger transcript, p. 294; McKean, *Ribbon Creek,* p. 25.

32. "Former Underwater Expert Recovers Sixth Body Thursday." *Beaufort Gazette,* Apr. 12, 1956, copy in GP–43–2.

33. Price interview.

CHAPTER 3

1. Brig. Gen. Samuel R. Shaw, Oral History Transcript (Oral History Collection, Marine Corps Historical Center, Washington, D.C.), p. 392, hereafter Shaw transcript; Lt. Gen. Joseph C. Burger, Oral History Transcript (Oral History Collection, Marine Corps Historical Center, Washington, D.C.), p. 291, hereafter Burger transcript.

2. Dept. of Defense news release, 8:00 P.M., Apr. 9, 1956 ("Ribbon Creek" file, Reference Section, Marine Corps Historical Center, Washington, D.C.).

3. Brig. Gen. James D. Hittle, Oral History Transcript (Oral History Collection, Marine Corps Historical Center, Washington, D.C.), p. 321, hereafter Hittle transcript; Gen. Wallace M. Greene, Jr., letter to author, May 22, 1982; Allan R. Millett, *Semper Fidelis: The History of the United States Marine Corps* (New York: Macmillan, 1980), p. 128, hereafter Millett, *Semper Fedelis.*

4. Shaw transcript, pp. 290–291.

5. Hittle transcript, p. 332.

6. Ibid., pp. 322–25.

7. Ibid.

8. Capt. Ralph C. Wood, "Summary of Events, 9–10 April 1956," ("Ribbon Creek" file, Reference Section, Marine Corps Historical Center, Washington, D.C.), hereafter Capt. R. C. Wood, "Summary."

9. Ibid.

10. Ibid.

11. "Drownings Attract Large Numbers of Newsmen," *Beaufort Gazette,* Apr. 12, 1956, copy in Greene Papers (Personal Papers Collection, Marine Corps Historical Center, Washington, D.C.), Box 43, Folder 1.

12. Brig. Gen. William B. McKean, *Ribbon Creek* (New York: Dial Press, 1958), p. 113, hereafter McKean, *Ribbon Creek.*

13. Capt. R. C. Wood, "Summary."

14. Burger transcript, p. 291.

15. Transcript of press interview with Gen. Pate, Apr. 10, 1956 ("Ribbon Creek" file, Reference Section, Marine Corps Historical Center, Washington, D.C.).

16. Shaw transcript, p. 293.

17. Ibid.

18. Ibid., p. 294.

19. Official biographical summary, Gen. Merrill B. Twining (Biographical files, Reference Section, Marine Corps Historical Center, Washington, D.C.); Gen. Merrill B. Twining, comments on draft ms., Apr. 8, 1984, hereafter Twining comments; Brig. Gen. Samuel R. Shaw, telephone comments on draft ms., Apr. 20, 1984; Millett, *Sempter Fidelis,* pp. 453–56.

20. Gen. Merrill B. Twining, Oral History Transcript (Oral History Collection, Marine Corps Historical Center, Washington, D.C.), hereafter Twining transcript. Used by special permission of Gen. Twining.

21. Shaw transcript, p. 294.

22. Hittle transcript, pp. 325–26.

23. Twining comments, p. 354.

24. Ibid.

25. Shaw transcript, p. 295.

26. Ibid.; "House Delays Marine Quiz," *New York Daily News,* Apr. 13, 1956; Albion B. Hailey, "Marines Fear Ease-Up on Boot Training," *Washington Post,* Apr. 15, 1956.

27. Hittle transcript, p. 325; Twining transcript, p. 353.

28. Hittle transcipt, p. 324.

29. Twining comments.

30. Hittle transcript, p. 324.

31. Shaw transcript, p. 295; Hittle transcript, p. 326.

32. Hittle transcript, pp. 325–26; Twining transcript, p. 353.

33. United Press International, "Court-Martial in 1954 Case," *New York Times,* Apr. 13, 1956; Associated Press, "Marine Court Hears Details of Tragedy," *Washington Post,* Apr. 12, 1956; Albion B. Hailey, "Marines Fear Ease-Up in Boot Training," *Washington Post,* Apr. 15, 1956; Anthony Leviero, "Marine Noncoms Caught in Middle," *New York Times,* Apr. 15, 1956; Anthony Leviero, "Marine Training—Theory and Practice," *New York Times,* Apr. 15, 1956.

34. Burger transcript, p. 34.

35. Official biographical sketch, Gen. Wallace M. Greene, Jr. (Biographical files, Reference Section, Marine Corps Historical Center, Washington, D.C.); McKean, *Ribbon Creek,* p. 177; author's observations.

36. Burger transcript, p. 295; Record of Proceedings, Court of Inquiry, ordered Apr. 9, 1956, with endorsements ("Ribbon Creek" file, Reference Section, Marine Corps Historical Center, Washington, D.C.).

37. Ibid.; Twining comments.

38. Hittle transcript, p. 326.

39. Ibid.

40. Ibid., pp. 326–27.

41. U.S. Congress, House, Committee on Armed Services, Hearing No. 76, "Report of the Commandant of the Marine Corps," May 1, 1956, *Hearings before the Committee on Armed Services, House of Representatives,* 84th Cong., 2d Sess., 1956, pp. 7157–60.

42. McKean, *Ribbon Creek,* p. 532.

43. Burger transcript, pp. 295, 301.

44. Shaw transcript, p. 301.

45. Ibid., p. 302.

46. Twining comments.

CHAPTER 4

1. Gen. Wallace M. Greene, Jr., letter to author, May 22, 1982.

2. Commandant of the Marine Corps (CMC) message, 011919Z May 57, "Instructions to New Commanding Generals of Recruit Training Commands," copy in Greene Papers (Personal Papers Collection, Marine Corps Historical Center, Washington, D.C.), Box 43, Folder 4, hereafter

GP with box and folder numbers (e.g., GP–43–4); "HQMC Briefing for Commanding Generals of Recruit Depots and Commanding Generals, Recruit Training Commands, 1 May 1956, " copy in GP–42–6.

3. CMC message, P022104Z May 57 to CG, 2d Marine Division, copy in GP–43–3; CG, 2d Marine Division orders, dated May 3, 1956, copy in GP–49–4; Gen. Wallace M. Greene, Jr., letter to author, May 22, 1982.

4. CG, 2d Marine Division messages, 031600Z May 56 and 031632Z May 56, copies in GP–43–7.

5. Gen. Wallace M. Greene, Jr., interview by author, Aug. 31, 1983.

6. CMC message 031035Z May 56 to Commander, Marine Corps Air Station, Cherry Point, N.C., copy in GP–43–3.

7. Brig. Gen. William B. McKean, *Ribbon Creek* (New York: Dial Press, 1958), p. 178, hereafter McKean, *Ribbon Creek*.

8. Brig. Gen. Wallace M. Greene, Jr., daily work sheets, May 4–June 22, 1956, copies in GP–42–5; Greene interview.

9. Gen. Wallace M. Greene, Jr., letter to Dr. Eugene Alvarez, Feb. 8, 1982, copy provided to author.

10. "Summary of the Comments of the Drill Instructors," notes from conference held at 2:00 P.M., May 5, 1956, copy in GP–42–3.

11. Gen. Wallace M. Greene, Jr., letter to author, May 22, 1982.

12. "Summary of the Comments of the Staff NCO Advisory Council," May 6, 1956, copy in GP–42–3.

13. Maj. Gen. George H. Cloud, Oral History Transcript, 1970 (Oral History Collection, Marine Corps Historical Center, Washington, D.C.).

14. Brig. Gen. Wallace M. Greene, Jr., letter to Maj. Gen. David M. Shoup, June 14, 1956, copy in GP–46–2.

15. Brig. Gen. Wallace M. Greene, Jr., "Notes on Telephone Conversation w/ Gen. Shoup, 7 May 56," copy in GP–42–3; Brig. Gen. Greene's work sheet for Thursday, May 8, 1956, copy in GP–42–5.

16. Brig. Gen. W. M. Greene, Jr., work sheet for Tuesday, May 8, 1956, copy in GP–42–5; Gen. W. M. Greene, Jr., letter to Dr. Eugene Alvarez, Mar. 23, 1982, copy supplied to author.

17. Brig. Gen. W. M. Greene, Jr., letter to author, Dec. 11, 1982.

18. Brig. Gen. W. M. Greene, Jr., work sheet for Tuesday, May 8, 1956, copy in GP–42–5.

19. Maj. Gen. D. M. Shoup, memo to Brig. Gens. Greene and Shapley, May 11, 1956, copy in GP–46–4.

20. Headquarters Marine Corps, "Recruit Training Survey, July 1956," copy in GP–46–2.

21. Bem Price, " 'Book' Is Sad Story to Marine Noncoms," *Washington Post,* May 27, 1956.

22. Ibid.

23. See GP–43 for the file of Bem Price's feature articles.

24. Capt. Mark P. Fennessy, memorandum, "Report on Visit to Parris Island," submiotted to Maj. Gen. D. M. Shoup, June 8, 1956, copy in GP–46–2.

25. Ibid.

26. Cloud transcript.

27. Brig. Gen. W. M. Greene, Jr., letter to Maj. Gen. D. M. Shoup, June 14, 1956; Inspector-General for Recruit Training report to CMC, July 12, 1956; and Brig. Gen. W. M. Greene, Jr., letter to Maj. Gen. D. M. Shoup, July 25, 1956. Copies in GP–46–2.

28. Brig. Gen. W. M. Greene, Jr., letter to Inspector-General for Recruit Training, June 30, 1956, copy in GP–46–22.

29. Fennessy report.

30. Capt. Robert R. Meeker, ms., "Fit to Fight," submitted to *Marine Corps Gazette,* Jan. 10, 1957, copy in GP–43–10; McKean, *Ribbon Creek,* p. 38.

31. Andrew St. George, "Has Tough Parris Island Gone Soft?" *Real* (March 1957), p. 17; Brig. Gen. W. M. Greene, Jr., letter to Maj. Gen. David M. Shoup, July 25, 1956, copy in GP–46–2.

32. Inspector-General for Recruit Training, memo to CMC, July 12, 1956, copy in GP–42–6.

33. Brig. Gen. W. M. Greene, Jr., letter to Maj. Gen. D. M. Shoup, July 25, 1956, copy in GP–42–6.

34. Ibid.

35. Ibid.; Col. R. T. Vance, draft staff study, "Actions of the RTC with Regard to the Trial of SSgt McKeon," n.d., copy in GP–41–2; Albion H. Hailey, "McKeon's Lawyer Claims Poll Shows Marine Training Sound," *Washington Post,* July 22, 1956.

36. Gen. W. M. Greene, Jr., letter to author, Dec. 11, 1982; Commanding General, RTC, Parris Island, letters to Inspector-General for Recruit Training, July 9 and 11, 1956, with handwritten replies by Maj. Gen. D. M. Shoup, both in GP–46–2.

37. Brig. Gen. W. M. Greene, Jr., letter to Maj. Gen. D. M. Shoup, July 10, 1956, copy in GP–46–4; Maj. Gen. D. M. Shoup, memo to Brig. Gen. W. M. Greene, Jr., July 12, 1956, copy in GP–46–2.

38. Director of Personnel, HQMC, office memo to Inspector-General for Recruit Training and Assistant Chief of Staff, G–3, dated July 12, 1956, with attached note by Maj. Gen. D. M. Shoup, copy in GP–46–4; Assistant Chief of Staff, G–3 memo to CMC, dated May 2, 1956, and memo to Chief of Staff, dated May 22, 1956, copies in office files of Chief of Staff, HQMC, for April–June 1956 (National Records Center, Suitland, Md., Accession No. 127–78–0022). Access to these records is controlled by Archives Section, Marine Corps Historical Center, Washington, D.C.

39. Brig. Gen. W. M. Greene, Jr., letter to Maj. Gen. D. M.

Shoup, May 18, 1956, copy in GP–46–4.

40. Brig. Gen. W. M. Greene, Jr., letter to Maj. Gen. D. M. Shoup, July 25, 1956, copy in GP–46–2. See also Cloud transcript.

41. Lester Bell, "DIs and GIs: What's Happening to the U.S. Marines?" *San Diego Union,* June 24, 1956; Maj. Gen. D. M. Shoup, letter to Brig. Gen. Alan Shapley, June 21, 1956; Brig. Gen. Alan Shapley, letter to Maj. Gen. D. M. Shoup, June 26, 1956. Copies of all in GP–46–4.

42. Brig. Gen. W. M. Greene, Jr., letter to Maj. Gen. D. M. Shoup, July 25, 1956, copy in GP–46–2.

43. Ibid.

CHAPTER 5

1. This chapter examines only those aspects of the McKeon court-material that illustrate the Marine Corps' institutional response to the Ribbon Creek incident. For a meticulous analysis of the trial's testimony and evidence, see Brig. Gen. William B. McKean, *Ribbon Creek* (New York: Dial Press, 1958).

2. Henry I. Shaw, Jr., Chief Historian, Marine Corps Historical Center, Washington, D.C., personal communication with author, June 1983.

3. "Ex-Marines to Aid Sgt. M. C. McKeon," Charleston, S.C., *News and Courier,* Apr. 19, 1956.

4. Albion C. Hailey, "Marines Fear Ease-Up in Boot Training," *Washington Post,* Apr. 15, 1956; and "McKeon's Lawyers Claim Poll Shows Marine Training Sound," *Washington Post,* July 22, 1956.

5. Joe McCarthy, "The Man Who Helped the Sergeant." *Life* (Aug. 13, 1956), p. 59.

6. Ibid., p. 52.

7. Ibid.

8. Linda Charlton, "Emile Zola Berman, 78, Dead; Defense Attorney for Sirhan," *New York Times,* July 5, 1981.

9. Lt. Col. Duane L. Faw, memo to CG, MCRD, Parris Island, dated June 30, 1956, copy in Greene Papers (Personal Papers Collection, Marine Corps Historical Center, Washington, D.C.), Box 43, Folder 9, hereafter cited as GP with box and folder number (e.g., GP–43–9).

10. Ibid. See also U.S. Congress, House, Committee on Armed Services, Hearing No. 76, "Report of the Commandment of the Marine Corps," May 1, 1956, *Hearings before the Committee on Armed Services, House of Representatives,* 84th Cong., 2d Sess., 1956, pp. 7157–60.

11. Brig. Gen. James D. Hittle, Oral History Transcript, 1976 (Oral History Collection, Marine Corps Historical Center, Washington, D.C.), p. 275, hereafter Hittle transcript.

12. Brig. Gen. William B. McKean, *Ribbon Creek* (New York:

Dial Press, 1968), p. 307, hereafter McKean, *Ribbon Creek.*

13. Lt. Gen. Vernon T. Megee, letter to Brig. Gen. Wallace M. Greene, Jr., Oct. 30, 1956, copy in GP–41–12.

14. McKean, *Ribbon Creek,* p. 307.

15. Hittle transcript, p. 329.

16. Ibid.

17. Brig. Gen. Samuel R. Shaw, Oral History Transcript, 1970 (Oral History Collection, Marine Corps Historical Center, Washington, D.C.), hereafter Shaw transcript.

18. CG, MCRD, Parris Island, letter to CMC, undated copy, in GP–46–5.

19. Lt. Col. Duane L. Faw, memo to CG, MCRD, Parris Island, dated June 30, 1956, copy in GP–43–9.

20. Col. Ralph C. Wood, memorandum for the record, "Phone Call from Lt. Col. Donald R. Nugent at 1545 This Date," dated July 6, 1956, copy in GP–44–2; Maj. Charles B. Sevier, memo to CG, MCRD, Parris Island, dated July 6, 1956, copy in GP–44–2; and CG, MCRD, Parris Island, memo to CMC, dated July 9, 1956, copy in GP–41–12.

21. CMC message to CG, MCRD, Parris Island, dated July 10, 1956, copy in GP–44–2.

22. CMC message to CG, MCRD, Parris Island, dated July 11, 1956, copy in GP–44–2.

23. Jim Bishop, "Officers Gagged on McKeon Aid by Parris Brass," *New York Journal American,* July 17, 1956; "News Release Policy from CMC, " N.D., copy in GP–44–2.

24. Transcript of pretrial conference, quoted in McKean, *Ribbon Creek,* pp. 278–79.

25. Joe McCarthy, "The Man Who Helped the Sergeant," *Life* (Aug. 13, 1956), p. 52, hereafter McCarthy, "The Man Who Helped the Sergeant."

26. McKean, *Ribbon Creek,* p. 372.

27. McCarthy, "The Man Who Helped the Sergeant," p. 52.

28. Albion H. Hailey, "McKeon's Lawyer Claims Poll Shows Marine Training Sound," *Washington Post,* July 22, 1956.

29. McCarthy, "The Man Who Helped the Sergeant," p. 52.

30. Ibid. See also McKean, *Ribbon Creek,* p. 344; and Hittle transcript, p. 330.

31. Shaw transcript, p. 201.

32. Brig. Gen. W. M. Greene, Jr., letter to Maj. Gen. D. M. Shoup, July 25, 1956, copy in GP–46–2.

33. Bem Price, "No Hate in Slapping Man, McKeon Says," *Atlanta Journal,* Sept. 1, 1956, copy in Bem Price Collection (Personal Papers Collection, Marine Corps Historical Center, Washington, D.C.).

34. Bem Price, "Marine Boss Says He Would 'Bust' McKeon and

Give Him Transfer," *Birminham News,* Aug. 1, 1956, copy in Bem Price Collection (Personal Papers Collection, Marine Corps Historical Center, Washington, D.C.).

35. Ibid.

36. Bem Price, "Puller Thinks Marine Corps Regrets Court-Martial of Sarge," *Brunswick Herald,* Aug. 2, 1956, copy in Bem Price Collection (Personal Papers Collection, Marine Corps Historical Center, Washington, D.C.).

37. Hittle transcipt, p. 333.

38. McCarthy, "The Man Who Helped the Sergeant," p. 51.

39. Ibid.

40. Shaw transcript, pp. 302–3; Secretary of the Navy, Court-Martial Order 1–56, dated Oct. 5, 1956, quoted in McKean, *Ribbon Creek,* pp. 527–31.

41. McKean, *Ribbon Creek,* p. 526.

42. Brig. Gen. W. M. Greene, Jr., letter to Maj. Gen. D. M. Shoupe, Oct. 19, 1956, copy in GP–42–1.

CHAPTER 6

1. Dr. Richard H. Bradford, letter to author, Apr. 29, 1980.

2. Recruit Training Command, Parris Island, "Standard Operating Procedures for Instruction-Inspection Section," dated July 26, 1956, copy in Greene Papers (Personal Papers Collection, Marine Corps Historical Center, Washington, D.C.), Box 44, Folder 8, cited hereafter as GP plus box and folder numbers (e.g., GP–44–8).

3. Recruit Training Command Order 6100.2A, dated Aug. 13, 1956, copy in GP–43–9.

4. Recruit Lesson Plans, Parris Island, S.C., copies in GP–44–1.

5. Capt. Robert R. Meeker, ms., "First to Fight," submitted to *Marine Corps Gazette,* Jan. 10, 1957, copy in GP–43–10.

6. Capt. F. S. Thomas, "New Approaches to Basic Training," *United States Naval Institute Proceedings* 83 (October 1957), p. 1045, hereafter Thomas, "New Approaches"; Brig. Gen. W. M. Greene, Jr., Armed Forces Day Speech, Beaufort, S.C., May 18, 1957; see also Mark W. Clark, *From the Danube to the Yalu* (New York: Harper, 1954) pp. 192–94. For a stronger viewpoint, see T. R. Fehrenbach, *This Kind of War: A Study in Unpreparedness* (New York: Simon & Schuster, 1963), passim.

7. Thomas, "New Approaches," p. 1045.

8. Ibid.

9. Ibid.

10. Ibid., p. 1054.

11. Brig. Gen. W. M. Greene, Jr., letter to Brig. Gen. Alpha L. Bowser, CG, RTC, San Diego, Feb. 27, 1957, copy in GP–45–15.

12. "Reactions of Recruits to Recruit Training," compiled at Headquarters Marine Corps, December 1956, copy in GP–42–6.

13. Brig. Gen. W. M. Greene, Jr., letter to Maj. Gen. D. M. Shoup, July 31, 1956, copy in GP–46–2; Food Service Director memo to Assistant Chief of Staff (AC/S), Marine Corps Recruit Depot Parris Island, dated Aug. 1, 1956, copy in GP–43–9; and National Research Council, *Recommended Daily Allowances* (Washington: National Academy of Science, 1974), p. 27.

14. Brig. Gen. W. M. Greene, Jr., letter to Brig. Gen. Alpha L. Bowser, CG, RTC, San Diego, dated January 21, 1957, copy in GP–45–15.

15. Commanding Officer, Weapons Training Battalion memo to CG, RTC, Parris Island, dated Oct. 3, 1956, copy in GP–43–9.

16. Jim G. Lucas, "Parris Island Boots Still Getting Works," *Washington Daily News,* Oct. 29, 1956, hereafter Jim Lucas, "Parris Island Boots"; M. Sgt. Paul Sarokin, "Parris Island"; *Leatherneck,* September 1956, pp. 15–16, hereafter Sarokin, "Parris Island"; Sgt. Rudy R. Dean, letter to editor, *Bellows Falls Times,* Mar. 14, 1957, copy in GP–42–11; Maj. Robert I. Edwards, interview, Mar. 19, 1981.

17. Sarokin, "Parris Island," p. 16.

18. Ibid., pp. 16–21; Jim G. Lucas, "Parris Island Boots."

19. Ralph Turtinan, "Things Have Changed in 'the Corps,' " *Minneapolis Star,* Sept. 17, 1956; see also Sarokin, "Parris Island," p. 20.

20. Brig. Gen. W. M. Greene, Jr., letter to Maj. Gen. D. M. Shoup, Sept. 19, 1956; Bem Price, "The Terror Is Gone," *Detroit Free Press,* Nov. 11, 1956, copy in Bem Price Collection (Personal Papers Collection, Marine Corps Historical Center, Washington, D.C.).

21. Brig. Gen. W. M. Greene, Jr., letter to editor, *Savannah Morning News,* Feb. 28, 1957.

22. MCRD Law Specialist, Memo to Maj. Gen. Litzenberg, dated Oct. 13, 1956, copy in GP–42–3.

23. Draft letter, CG, RTC to CG, MCRD, Parris Island, n.d., copy in GP–42–3.

24. Ibid.

25. Asst. Chief of Staff (G–3), memo to CMC, dated May 25, 1956, copy in HQMC office files, Suitland National Records Center, Suitland, Md. (Accession No. 127–78–0022), access available through Archives Section, Marine Corps Historical Center, Washington, D.C.

26. Brig. Gen. W. M. Greene, Jr., letter to Maj. Gen. D. M. Shoup, Sept. 6, 1956, copy in GP–46–2.

27. Maj. Gen. D. M. Shoup, letter to Brig. Gen. W. M. Greene, Jr., Sept.10, 1956, copy in GP–46–4; Asst. Chief of Staff (G–4), memo to CG, RTC, Parris Island, dated Sept. 21, 1956, copy in GP–43–2.

28. Brig. Gen. W. M. Greene, Jr., letter to Maj. Gen. D. M. Shoup, Oct. 1, 1956, copy in GP–46–2.

29. CG, RTC, Letter to CG, MCRD, Parris Island, dated Oct. 25, 1956, copy in GP–43–9.

30. Ibid.

31. CG, MCRD, Parris Island, return endorsement, dated Nov. 10, 1956, to CG, RTC's letter to CG, MCRD, Parris Island, on "Recreational and Athletic Equipment for Recruits, Request for Purchase of," dated Oct. 25, 1956.

32. CG, RTC, Parris Island, letter to CMC, dated Jan. 25, 1957, "Officer Personnel, Relief of," copy in GP–43–10.

33. CMC, letter to CG, RTC, Parris Island, dated Mar. 7, 1956, copy in GP–43–10.

34. CMC, letter to CG, RTC, and CG, MCRD, Parris Island, "Organization of Marine Corps Recruit Depots," dated Feb. 13, 1957, copy in GP–43–10.

CHAPTER 7

1. Brig. Gen. Wallace M. Greene, Jr., letters to Maj. Gen. David M. Shoup, dated Aug. 7 and 11, 1956, copies in Greene Papers (Personal Papers Collection, Marine Corps Historical Center, Washington, D.C.) Box 42, Folder 1, hereafter GP with box and folder number (e.g., GP–42–1). See also letter to Maj. Gen. Shoup, dated Aug. 9, 1956, copy in GP–46–2.

2. Brig. Gen. W. M. Greene, Jr., letter to Maj. Gen. D. M. Shoup, Sept. 6, 1956, copy in GP–46–2.

3. Lt. Col. John R. Blandford, USMCR, memo to CMC, dated Sept. 26, 1956, with HQMC staff comments (Archives, Marine Corps Historical Center, Washington, D.C.).

4. Ibid.

5. Director, 6th Marine Corps Reserve and Recruitment District, letter to Brig. Gen. W. M. Greene, Jr., n.d., copy in GP–44–6.

6. "Public Relations" folder, copy in GP–43–24.

7. Ibid.

8. Allan R. Millett, *The American Political System and Civilian Control of the Military: A Historical Perspective,* Mershon Center Position Papers in the Policy Sciences, No. 4 (Columbus: The Mershon Center of the Ohio State University, 1979), p. 55; Bem Price, interview Jan. 17, 1983, hereafter Price interview.

9. "Summary," delivered to the Secretary of the Navy, Mar. 14, 1957, by the Associated Press Washington Bureau, copy in GP–42–1, hereafter Associated Press, "Summary."

10. Bem Price, "The Terror Is Gone," *Detroit Free Press,* Nov. 11, 1956, copy in GP–42–8.

11. Bem Price, "U.S. Marines Reduce Trials to a 'Farce,' Reporter Writes,'' Charleston, S.C., *News and Courier,* Mar. 4, 1957, copy in GP–42–8.

12. Brig. Gen. W. M. Greene, Jr., letter to Gen. Randolph McC. Pate, dated Mar. 30, 1957, copy in GP–42–1.

13. Brig. Gen. W. M. Greene, Jr., leter to Gen. R. McC. Pate, dated Mar. 8, 1956, copy in GP–42–1.

14. Brig. Gen. W. M. Greene, Jr., letter to Gen. R. McC. Pate, dated Mar. 30, 1956, copy in GP–42–1.

15. Brig. Gen. W. M. Greene, Jr., letter to Gen. R. McC. Pate, dated Mar. 4, 1956, copy in GP–41–12.

16. Jay Lewis, "Reds in TV, Press, Radio, Senators Say," *Washington Post,* Mar. 3, 1957, copy in GP–42–8.

17. CG, RTC, Parris Island, letter to CG, Marine Corps Base (MCB), Camp Lejeune, N.C., et al, dated Mar. 6, 1956, copy in GP–41–12.

18. Brig. Gen. W. M. Greene, Jr., letter to Gen. R. McC. Pate, dated Mar. 9, 1956, copy in GP–43–8.

19. CG, RTC, Parris Island, letter to all commanding officers at Parris Island, dated Mar. 10, 1957, copy in GP–42–8; Brig. Gen. W. M. Greene, Jr., letter to Mr. William L. Beale, Jr., Chief, Washington Bureau of the Associated Press, dated April 7, 1957, copy in GP–42–11.

20. Press Release, MCRD, Parris Island, dated Mar. 9, 1957, copy in GP–43–7.

21. Director of Information, HQMC, memo to CMC, dated Mar. 22, 1957. See also Associated Press, "Summary," delivered to Secretary of the Navy on Mar. 14, 1957. Copies of both in GP–42–1. Price interview, Jan. 17, 1983.

22. Gen. R. McC. Pate, letter to Brig. Gen. W. M. Greene, Jr., dated Mar. 12, 1957, copy in GP–41–12.

23. Gen. R. McC. Pate, letter to Brig. Gen. W. M. Greene, Jr, dated Mar. 26, 1957; Director of Information, HQMC, memo to CMC, dated Mar. 22, 1957. Copies of both are in GP–42–1.

24. Gen. R. McC. Pate, letter to Brig. Gen. W. M. Greene, Jr., dated Mar. 20, 1957, copy in GP–42–1.

25. Ibid.

26. CMC letter signed by N.E. McKonly (by direction), to Brig. Gen. W. M. Greene, Jr., dated Mar. 22, 1957, copy in GP–43–7; photocopy of fitness report on Brig. Gen. W. M. Greene, Jr., completed by Gen. R. McC. Pate, dated Mar. 1, 1957, copy in GP–49–2.

27. Brig. Gen. W. M. Greene, Jr., draft message to CMC, n.d., with Brig. Gen. Greene's handwritten notation, "Never sent," copy in GP–49–2.

28. Brig. Gen. W. M. Greene, Jr., letter to Gen. R. McC. Pate, Mar. 30, 1957, copy in GP–42–1.

29. " 'Boot Camp' Memento," Parris Island *Boot,* May 31, 1957, copy in GP–44–9.

CHAPTER 8

1. Gen. Wallace M. Greene, Jr., interview, Aug. 31, 1983.

2. Lt. Gen. Robert H. Barrow, testimony, *Hearings on Marine Recruit Training and Recruiting Programs,* House Armed Services Committee (Washington, D.C.: Government Printing Office, 1976), pp. 210–13.

3. Gen. W. M. Greene, Jr., letter to author, dated Dec. 11, 1982.

4. Allan R. Millett, *Semper Fidelis: The History of the United States Marine Corps* (New York: Macmillan, 1980), p. 523.

5. Edwin McDowell, *To Keep Our Honor Clean* (New York: Vanguard Press, 1980), pp. 147–48.

6. Lt. Gen. John R. Chaisson, transcript, "Briefing for Secretary of the Navy's Advisory Committee, Headquarters Marine Corps, March 23, 1972" (Oral History Collection, Marine Corps Historical Center, Washington, D.C.), p. 346, hereafter Chaisson transcript.

7. Don A. Schance, "Return of the Old Breed," *Esquire,* January 1961, p. 118, copy in biographical file on Gen. David M. Shoup (Reference Section, Marine Corps Historical Center, Washington, D.C.).

8. Advertisement, Classified Section, *Army–Navy–Air Force Register and Defense Times,* Nov. 5, 1960, p. 45.

9. Gen. Wallace M. Greene, Jr., letter to author, May 22, 1982; copy in Gen. Greene's personal papers (Personal Papers Collection, Marine Corps Historical Center, Washington, D.C.).

10. "Where Are They Now?: M. C. McKeon and the 1956 Parris Island Tragedy," *Newsweek,* Aug. 17, 1970, p. 12.

11. Richard Pearson, "Emile Zola Berman Dies, Defended RFK's Assassin," *Washington Post,* July 5, 1981; Linda Charlton, "Emile Zola Berman, 78, Dead; Defense Attorney for Sirhan," *New York Times,* July 5, 1981.

12. Chaisson transcript, p. 346.

13. McKean, *Ribbon Creek* (New York: Dial Press, 1958), p. 534.

Bibliography

I. PRIMARY SOURCES

  A. ARCHIVAL SOURCES AND PRIVATE PAPERS

    1. Greene, General Wallace M., Jr., Personal Papers Collection, Marine Corps Historical Center, Washington, D.C., especially the following categories:

      a. Correspondence. Boxes 16, 17, 45, 46.

      b. Daily Diary (notebook). Box 9.

      c. Investigations. Box 40.

      d. Newspaper and Magazine Clippings. Boxes 40, 42, 48.

      e. Parris Island Files. Boxes 42–48, 51.

      f. Photograph Collections. Boxes 46, 48.

      g. Public Relations. Box 41.

      h. Reports. Box 41.

      i. Ribbon Creek Incident, Box 42.

      j. Transfer Orders. Box 49.

      k. Unit Journals (May 4, 1956–April 1957). Boxes 1–4.

    2. Official Files

      a. Chief of Staff, Headquarters, Marine Corps, office files, April–June 1956 (National Records Center, Suitland, Md., Accession No. 127–78–0022). Access to these official records is available through the Archives Section, Marine Corps Historical Center, Washington, D.C.

      b. Commandant of the Marine Corps, office files, 1956 (National Records Center, Suitland, Md., Accession No. 127–78–0022). Access to these official records is available through the Archives Section, Marine Corps Historical Center, Washington, D.C.

      c. Blandford, Lt. Col. John R., Memorandum to Commandant of the Marine Corps, Sept. 26, 1956, with HQMC staff comments (Archives Section, Marine Corps Historical Center, Washington, D.C.).

3. Unofficial Files

    a. Biographical Files, Reference Section, Marine Corps Historical Center, Washington, D.C.

    b. "Ribbon Creek" file, Reference Section, Marine Corps Historical Center, Washington, D.C.

B. ORAL HISTORY MEMOIRS

The following transcripts of oral history interviews are available at the Marine Corps Historical Center, Washington, D.C. Unless otherwise noted, these interviews are open to scholars.

Burger, Lt. Gen. Joseph C.

Chaisson, Lt. Gen. John R.

Cloud, Maj. Gen. George H.

Hittle, Brig. Gen. James D.

Paradis, Mr. Don V.

Shaw, Brig. Gen. Samuel R.

Twining, Gen. Merrill B., closed, used by permission.

C. CORRESPONDENCE AND INTERVIEWS

Edwards, Maj. Robert I., telephone interview, Mar. 19, 1981.

Greene, Gen. Wallace M., Jr., interview, Aug. 31, 1983.

———, letter to Dr. Eugene Alvarez, Feb. 8, 1982, copy provided courtesy of Gen. Greene.

———, letter to author, May 22, 1982.

———, letter to author, Dec. 11, 1982.

Price, Bem, interview, Jan. 17, 1983.

Shaw, Henry I., Jr. (Chief Historian, Marine Corps Historical Center), personal communication, June 1983.

Shaw, Brig. Gen. Samuel R., comments to author, via telephone, on draft ms., Apr. 20, 1984.

Twining, Gen. Merrill B., letter to author, comments on draft ms., Apr. 8, 1984.

D. NEWSPAPER ARTICLES

Associated Press, "Marine Court Hears Details of Tragedy," *Washington Post,* Apr. 12, 1956.

Bell, Lester, "DIs and GIs: What's Happening to the U.S. Marines?" *San Diego Union,* June 24, 1956.

Bishop, Jim, "Officers Gagged on McKeon Aid by Parris Brass," *New York Journal American,* July 17, 1956.

" 'Boot Camp' Memento," Parris Island *Boot,* May 31, 1957.

"Boystown Marine Related Experience in Death March," Arlington, N.J., *Observer,* May 17, 1956. Copy in Greene Papers, Box 42, Folder 12 (Personal Papers Collections, Marine Corps Historical Center, Washington, D.C.).

Dean, Sgt. Rudy R., letter to editor, *Bellows Falls Times,* Mar.

14, 1957. Copy in Greene Papers, Box 42, Folder 11 (Personal Papers Collections, Marine Corps Historical Center, Washington, D.C.).

"Drownings Attract Large Numbers of Newsmen," *Beaufort Gazette,* Apr. 12, 1956.

"Ex-Marines to Aid Sgt. M. C. McKeon," Charleston, S.C., *News and Courier,* Apr. 19, 1956.

"Former Underwater Expert Recovers Sixth Body Thursday," *Beaufort Gazette,* Apr. 12, 1956.

Greene, Brig. Gen. Wallace M., Jr., letter to editor, Savannah, Ga., *Morning News,* Feb. 28, 1956.

Hailey, Albion B., "Marines Fear Ease-Up in Boot Training," *Washington Post,* Apr. 15, 1956.

———, "McKeon's Lawyer Claims Poll Shows Marine Training Sound," *Washington Post,* July 22, 1956.

"House Delays Marine Quiz," *New York Daily News,* Apr. 13, 1956.

Leviero, Anthony, "Marines Noncoms Caught in Middle," *New York Times,* Apr. 15, 1956.

———, "Marine Training: Theory and Practice," *New York Times,* Apr. 15, 1956.

Lewis, Jay, "Reds in TV, Press, Radio, Senators Say," *Washington Post,* Mar. 3, 1957.

Lucas, Jim G., "Parris Island Boots Still Getting Works," *Washington Daily News,* Oct. 29, 1956.

McLane, Col. Merrill F., letter to editor, *Washington Post,* Dec. 2, 1980.

"Marine Corps Puts the Blame," *Washington Star,* May 16, 1956.

"Marine Court of Inquiry Conducting Daily Secret Hearings on Sunday's Death March," *Beaufort Gazette,* Apr. 12, 1956.

O'Leary, Jeremiah,"At Parris Island: The Summers of '42 and '72," *Washington Star,* June 25, 1972.

Price, Bem, " 'Book' Is Sad Story to Marine Noncoms," *Washington Post,* May 27, 1956.

———, "McKeon Court-Martial Stirs 'Spit-and-Polish' Marine Post," *Columbus Dispatch,* July 22, 1956.

———, "Marine Boss Says He Would 'Bust' McKeon and Give Him Transfer," *Birmingham News,* Aug. 1, 1956. Copy in Bem Price Papers (Personal Papers Collections, Marine Corps Historical Center, Washington, D.C.).

———, "No Hate in Slapping Man, McKeon says," *Atlanta Journal,* Sept. 1, 1956. Copy in Bem Price Papers (Personal Papers Collections, Marine Corps Historical Center, Washington, D.C.).

———, "The Terror Is Gone," *Detroit Free Press,* Nov. 11, 1956.

———, "U.S. Marines Reduce Trials to a 'Farce,' Reporter Writes," Charleston, S.C., *News and Courier,* Mar. 4, 1957.

Special Correspondent, "Six Marine Drill Instructors Convicted of Maltreatment," Charleston, S.C., *News and Courier,* Mar. 4, 1957.

Turtinan, Ralph, "Things Have Changed in 'The Corps,' " *Minneapolis Star,* Sept. 17, 1956.

————, "Marines Change Tactics, Not Goals," *Minneapolis Star,* Sept. 18, 1956.

United Press International, "Court-Martial in 1954 Case," *New York Times,* Apr. 13, 1956.

E. MAGAZINES

Bartlett, Tom, "Conversations with a Brew," *Leatherneck,* Aug. 1972.

Blair, Clay, Jr., "The Tragedy of Platoon 71 Puts Marine Training under Fire," *Life,* Apr. 23, 1956.

Finan, James, "The Making of a Leatherneck," *American Mercury,* April 1951.

Kauffman, Mark, "How to Make Marines," *Life,* Oct. 3, 1951.

McCarthy, Joe, "The Man Who Helped the Sergeant," *Life,* Aug. 13, 1956.

Smith, Maj. Robert A., "First to Fight," *Marine Corps Gazette* 60 (November 1976).

F. BOOKS

McKean, Brig. Gen. William B. *Ribbon Creek.* New York: Dial Press, 1958.

Paige, Col. Mitchell, *A Marine Named Mitch.* New York: Vantage Press, 1975.

G. GOVERNMENT DOCUMENTS

U.S. Congress, House, Committee on Armed Services, *Hearings on Marine Corps Recruit Training and Recruiting Programs.* 94th Cong., 2d Sess., 1976.

————, *Hearings before the Committee on Armed Services.* Hearing No. 76, "Report of the Commandant of the Marine Corps," May 1, 1956. 84th Cong., 2d Sess., 1956.

II. SECONDARY SOURCES

A. Books

Champie, Elmore A. *A Brief History of the Marine Corps Recruit Depot, Parris Island, South Carolina, 1891–1962.* Washington, D.C.: Headquarters, U.S. Marine Corps, 1962.

Clark, Gen. Mark W. *From the Danube to the Yalu.* New York: Harper, 1954.

Farb, Peter. *Man's Rise to Civilization.* Man's Rise to Civilization. New York: Avon, 1973.

Fehrenbach, T. R. *This Kind of War: A Study in Unpreparedness.* New York: Simon & Schuster, 1963.

Greenway, John, *The Inevitable Americans,* New York: Alfred A. Knopf, 1964.

Janowitz, Morris, "Changing Patterns of Organizational Authority: The Military Establishment," *Administrative Science Quarterly* (March 1959), pp. 474–93; reprinted in Janowitz, Morris. *Military Conflict: Essays in the Institutional Analysis of War and Peace*. Beverly Hills: Sage Publications, 1975.

———, and Roger Little. *Sociology and the Military Establishment*. Beverly Hills: Sage Publications, 1974.

McDowell, Edwin, *To Keep Our Honor Clean* (a Novel). New York: Vanguard Press, 1980.

Manchester, William. *Goodbye Darkness: A Memoir of the Pacific War*. Boston: Little, Brown & Co., 1980.

Maris, Jesse C. *Remembering*. Privately printed, 1951.

Marshall, S. L. A. *Men Against Fire: The Problem of Battle Command in Future War,* reprint ed. Gloucester: Peter Smith, 1978.

Millett, Allan R. *The American Political System and Civillian Control of the Military: A Historical Perspective*. Mershon Center Position Papers in the Policy Sciences, No. 4, Columbus: The Mershon Center of the Ohio State University, 1979.

———, *Semper Fidelis: The History of the United States Marine Corps*. New York: Macmillan, 1980.

Moskin, Robert. *The U.S. Marine Corps Story*. New York: McGraw-Hill, 1977.

Nash, Gary B. *Red, White, and Black: The Peoples of Early America*. Englewood Cliffs, N.J.: Prentice-Hall, 1974.

National Research Council, *Recommended Daily Allowances*. Washington, D.C.: National Academy of Sciences, 1974.

Segal, David R. "Leadership and Management: Organization and Theory," in *Military Leadership,* ed. James A. Buck, and Lawrence J. Korb. Beverly Hills: Sage Publications, 1981.

Stouffer, Samuel A.; Arthur A. Lumsdaine; Marion H. Lumsdaine; Robin W. Williams, Jr.,; M. Brewster Smith; Irving L. Janis; Shirley A. Star; and Leonard S. Cottrell. *The American Soldier: Adjustment during Army Life,* vol. 1. Princeton: Princeton University Press, 1949.

———, *The American Soldier: Combat and Its Aftermath,* vol. 2. Princeton: Princeton University Press, 1949.

Thomason, John W. K, Jr. "Hate," In *And a Few Marines*. New York: Scribners, 1943.

Van Riper, Maj. Paul K.; Maj. Michael W. Wydo; and Maj. Donald P. Brown. *An Analysis of Marine Corps Training*. Newport: Naval War College Center for Advanced Research, 1978.

B. Articles

Allan, Henry, "The Corps," *Washington Post,* Mar. 5, 1972.

Charlton, Linda, "Emile Zola Berman, 78, Dead; Defense Attorney for Sirhan," *New York Times,* July 5, 1981.

Jones, Mel, "A New Look at MC Boot Camp Today: New

Devotion to Some Old Ways," *Navy Times,* May 31, 1976.

MacGillivray, George, "Historic Guadalcanal Maps in Collection," *Fortitudine,* Spring–Summer, 1982.

Middleton, Drew, "Rallying the Marines," *New York Times Magazine,* Dec. 4, 1983.

Pearson, Richard, "Emile Zola Berman Dies; Defended RFK's Assassin," *Washington Post,* July 5, 1981.

Polete, Harry, "Never the Twain Shall Meet . . . ," *Leatherneck,* August 1948.

St. George, Andrew, "Has Tough Parris Island Gone Soft?" *Real,* March 1957.

Sarokin, M. Sgt. Paul, "Parris Island," *Leatherneck,* September, 1956.

Schance, Don S., "Return of the Old Breed," *Esquire,* January 1961.

Thomas, Capt. Frederick S., "New Approaches to Recruit Training," *United States Naval Institute Proceedings* 83 (October 1957).

"Where Are They Now: M. C. McKeon and the 1956 Parris Island Tragedy," *Newsweek,* Aug. 17, 1970, p. 12.

Index

American citizen armies, characteristics of, 90
American public opinion, 113
American society, 4, 103, 110
Ammunition expenditure, 7
Amphibious warfare, 7
Annual Reserve duty, 101
Aranda, the (Australian aboriginal group), 5
Arlington, Va., 56
Armitage, Pvt. Francis, 36
Army General Classification Test, 21
Army, U.S. *See* U.S. Army
Article 37, UCMJ, 80
Associated Press, 38, 39, 63, 104–105, 107–108, 110
Augusta, Ga., 33, 37
Authority of NCOs and DIs, 96

Bare, Maj. Gen. Robert O., 70
Barracks 761, 33–34
Barrow, Gen. Robert H., 16, 26
Bartlett, Tom, 18
Base housing, 64–65
Battalion commanders, 20, 88
Bayonet fighting, 16
Beale, William L., Jr., 107–108
Beaufort, S.C., 38, 43, 58, 65, 72, 119
Behavior modification in recruit training, 88
Belt line, use of, in training, 4, 12–13
Berman, Emile Zola, 75–86, 120
Black drill instructors, 26
Blandford, John R., 48, 52–53, 101–102
Bonnett, Joyce E., xiii
Boot camp, 4–5, 8–10, 111–112
Boot leave, 78
Bradford, Prof. Richard H., 87–88
Breckinridge Trophy, 29
Bremerton, Wash., 10

Brewer, Pvt. Lewis, 36
Bronze Star Medal, 32, 104
Buckets, use of, in hazing, 11
Building AS-33, Page Field, Parris Island, 98
Bureau of Aeronautics, 98
Burger, Lt. Gen. Joseph C., 25, 27–29, 32–33, 37–38, 40, 43, 46, 49–51, 53, 83, 119
Buse, Lt. Gen. Henry W., Jr., xiv, 32, 37–38, 71

Caloric intake of recruits, 92
Camp Lejeune, N.C., 7, 56, 58, 61, 68, 70, 78, 108
Camp Matthews, Calif., 92
Camp Pendleton, Calif., 46, 55, 99
Campaign issues, 49
Capitol Hill, 41–42, 48–49, 52
Carolina Low Country, 11, 25
Chaisson, Lt. Gen. John R., 118, 121
Charlotte, N.C., 38
Cherry Point, N.C., 86
Chief of staff, 41, 56–57, 80
China, 29, 62
Church services, 33–34
Cigarettes and recruits, 11, 16, 87–88
Citizen-soldiers, 23
Close order drill, 10, 15–16
Clothing inspections, 13
Cloud, Col. George H., 71
Coercion of recruits, 20
Cohesion, 7–8
Cold War, 1–2
"Collaboration" by POWs in Korean War, 90
Combat Correspondents Program, 15
Combat efficiency, 8, 13
Combat success, 4
Combat survival, 9

Combat training, 3, 8
Combat veterans, 7, 18
Command influence over
    courts-martial, 84
Commandant of the Marine Corps, 16,
    19, 25, 28–29, 39, 40–41, 46, 48–55,
    78, 80, 84, 99–102, 108, 111, 120–121
Commissioned officers, 2, 6, 15, 20, 22,
    24–25, 31, 57, 87
Communism, instruction about, 91
Communist subversive activity,
    106–107, 110, 113, 117–118
Company commanders, 23
Conditioning platoon, Special Training
    Company, 67, 68
Congress, U.S., xii, 26, 41, 47–48,
    54–55, 74, 84, 115–116
Congressional armed services
    committees. See House Armed
    Services Committee; Senate Armed
    Services Committee
Congressional correspondence, 46
Congressional investigation, 47, 53–54,
    101, 113
Congressional liaison officer, 84
Congressmen, 19, 46
Contact relief by officers, 99
Corporal punishment, 5, 11, 15–16, 18,
    20, 26–27, 62
Corrective action versus punishment,
    96
Costello, Thomas P., 76
Court of inquiry, 44, 50–52
Courts-martial, 20, 27, 59, 94–95,
    104–105, 116
Crawford, Danny J., xiii
Culpable negligence, 51

Damage-limiting response, 115
Darden, William, 48
Deactivation of Fleet Marine Force
    units, 97
Deactivation of units, 99
Defense budget, 42
Defense counsel, 74
Dejarnette, David L., xii
Department of Defense, 106–107
Depot Sports Center, 66
Depot Recreation Council, 98
DI Advisory Council, 60, 69, 72, 93
Director of Personnel, HQMC, 70
Discipline, 4–9, 11, 31, 44, 57
Dominican Republic, 7
Double-timing, 24

Draft, xi, 6, 26, 90
Draftees, 26
Dreyfus case, 75–77, 85
Drill instructors: characteristics, 65;
    concerns of 22, 59, 66, 93; living
    quarters, 33, 64
Drill instructors School, 17, 21, 30, 51,
    57, 65, 70, 94
Duck walking, 24
Dutton, M. Sgt. Benjamin F., 58–59

Editors, role of, 38–39
Eisenhower Administration, 1, 42, 69
Eisenhower, President Dwight D., 120
Elbows and toes (punishment), 24
Englander, Evelyn A., xiii
Extension of recruit training, 97
Extra training, 24

Far East, 119
Faw, Lt. Col. Duane L., 51, 77–78
Federal Bureau of Investigation, 106,
    118
Feher, Pfc. Michael, 7
Fennessy, Capt. Mark P., 65–66
Ferrigno, M. Sgt. William G., 58–59.
    64, 72
Field hats, 72, 111
"Field day," 16, 33
Fire teams, 7
Fists, use of, 11, 15, 27
Fitness reports, 109, 116
Fleet Marine Force 2, 7, 16, 97, 102
Fleming, Joanna M., xiv
Fleming, John W., xiv
Fleming, Kathryn H., xiv
Food requirements of recruits, 91–92
Food service system, 92
Football, 6, 29
Footlocker, 11, 18, 30
Forced marches, 16
Frank, Benis M., xiii
Free laundry for DIs, 64
Funk, Col. Glenn C., 57–58, 61, 92–93

"GI party," 33
Gag rule, 79–80
Garroway, Dave, 76
Gates, Under Secretary of the Navy
    Thomas S., 84
General Classification Test (GCT), 21
General court-martial, 20, 60
"Goon platoon," 71
Grabowski, Pvt. Thomas, 36

Grand jury, military equivalent of, 51
Great Depression, 12, 16, 90
Greene, Gen. Wallace M., Jr., xiii–xiv, 12, 27, 50, 54, 56–57, 59, 62, 64, 67, 69, 71, 83, 87–88, 92–94, 96–97, 99–100, 102, 105–106, 108, 109–111, 115–117, 120–121
Greenway, John, 5
Guadalcanal, 13, 32
Guard duty, 33

Haircuts, 16
Hardeman, Pvt. Thomas C., 36, 39
Hazing, 4, 11, 15, 17–18, 20, 59. *See also* Maltreatment.
Headquarters Marine Corps (HQMC), 17, 19, 32, 40, 42, 45, 47, 51, 56–57, 62, 69, 75, 78, 82, 85, 87, 97–101, 115, 117–119
Heat casualties, 68, 71, 89
Heinl, Col. Robert D., 48
Helicopter doctrine development, 46
Helmet liners, 68
Historical Center (USMC), xiii
History of the U.S., instruction about, 91
Hittle, B. Gen. James D., 41–42, 46–48, 52–53, 78, 84
Hogaboom, Maj. Gen. Robert E. 85
"Honor platoon," 69
Hoover, J. Edgar, 118
Hospital Platoon, Special Training Company, 67
House Armed Services Committee, 41–42, 47, 49, 51–52, 78, 101
Housing, Parris Island area, S.C. 24
Howard, Maj. Gen. Samuel, 19
Huff, S. Sgt. Edward A., 31
Huizenga, Col. Richard M., 57–58, 66
Human relations, 4

IGMC. *See* Inspector General of the Marine Corps
Illicit financial dealings, 14, 27, 94, 104
Inchon, Korea, 112
Individual Combat Training, 66, 78
Infantry Training Regiment, 3, 61, 66
Infantry units, 6–7, 9, 30
Infantrymen, 3
Inspection section, 63
Inspector-General of the Marine Corps, 19, 99
Inspector-General for Recruit Training, 54, 61, 99, 115–116

Institutional backwaters, 25
Institutional reform, xii
Institutionalizing reform, 87–100
Instruction-Inspection Section, 88
Integration of the Services, 26
International News Service, 43
Investigation of citizens' group, 105–106
Investigations, types of, 95
Island-hopping campaigns, 7
Issuing of additional uniforms, 62
Iwo Jima monument, Parris Island, S.C., 24

Kennedy, Sen. Robert F., 120
King, Sgt. Richard J., 31, 33, 51
Kinkaid, Adm. Thomas C., 18
Korean War, xi–xiii, 1–2, 4, 8–9, 17–20, 25–26, 42, 46, 90, 104, 112–113
Krag-Jorgensen rifle, 10
Krulak, Lt. Gen. Victor H., 54

"Laying on of hands," 26
Leadership, 4, 6–7, 21, 64
Legal officer, Parris Island, 77
Legal system. *See* Uniform Code of Military Justice
Legion of Merit, 104
Length of recruit training, 20, 97
Lesson plans, 51, 89
Levine, Mrs. Clara, 76
Lexington, Va., 40
Life Magazine, 20, 25, 73
Litzenberg, Maj. Gen. Homer H., 61, 65, 78, 95–96, 98, 102
Long, Sen. Russell, 48
Los Angeles, Calif., 46
Low Country, 25
Lynch, Justice Walter A. (N.Y. Supreme Court), 75

Machine gun platoon, 30
Male initiation ceremonies, 5, 112
Maltreatment, 4, 5, 9, 11, 17–21, 23–24, 27, 29, 46–47, 49, 59, 87, 94, 101, 104, 107, 110, 114, 117–118; definition of, 4
Manchester, William, 15–16
Manslaughter, 51
Manual of arms, 10
Marine Barracks, Parris Island, S.C., 17
Marine Barracks, Washington, D.C., 46

Marine Corps Air Station, Beaufort, S.C., 65, 72
Marine Corps Reserve, 70
Marksmanship, 13
Marksmanship coach, 33
Marshall, S. L. A., 8
Marshes. *See* Tidal marshes
Masters Golf Tournament, 33
McDowell, Edwin, 9, 114
McKean, B. Gen. William B., 18, 24–25, 30, 32–33, 43–44, 51, 53, 121
McKeon, S. Sgt. Matthew C., 31, 33, 35–38, 44–45, 50, 55, 63, 72, 120
McKeon Court-Martial, 72, 74–87
McLane, Col. M. F., 13
McLean, Va., 108
McNally, Justice James B. M. (N.Y. Supreme Court), 75
Medal of Honor, 54, 62
Medical Corps, USN, 119
Megee, Gen. Vernon E., 41–42, 46, 70, 85
Military history, xii
Military/Press relations, 103
Miller, J. Michael, xiii
Millett, Allan R., xiii
"Mixmaster" program in Vietnam War, 7
Mobilization, effects of, 14
Model for crisis reaction, 112
M-1 rifle, 20
Morale, 4
Morgan, Patricia E., xiii
Motivation Platoon, Special Training Company, 67, 68, 71

NCO. *See* Noncommissioned officers
National Broadcasting Company, 72–73
Navy Annex, 40, 56
Navy Department, 84
Navy, U.S. *See* U.S. Navy
New River air facility, 58
New York City, 10, 86, 120
New York State Supreme Court, 75
New York Times, 53
News media, 3, 39, 42–44, 48, 50, 55, 72, 78, 80, 95, 103–104
Newspaper editors, 38–39
Newsweek Magazine, 120
Night marches, 44, 50
Night training exercise, 42
Noncommissioned officers (NCO), xii, 4, 7, 9–10, 15, 17, 20–21, 23, 33, 50, 57–59, 64, 70, 75; concerns, 114

Norfolk, Va., 78, 82
Norms of behavior, 8
Nuclear deterrent, xi, 1
Nugent, Lt. Col. Donald R., 78
Numbering of recruit platoons, 31

Obedience, immediate, 4, 6
Obstacle courses, 69
Off-base housing, 65
Officer of the day, 25, 33, 37
Officer supervision, 24, 25
O'Leary, Jeremiah, 15–16
Opinion polls, 25, 26
Oppression of recruits, 51

Page Field, Parris Island, S.C., 65
Paige, Col. Mitchell "Mitch," 12–14
Parade field, 24
Paradis, Don V., 11
Parris Island, changes in title, 17
Pate, Gen. Randolph M., 28–29, 39–41, 43–46, 49, 51–53, 55–56, 69, 74–75, 77–78, 82–84, 99, 105, 107–108, 115–117, 119–120
Patrick, Capt. Charles, 37
Patriotism, 16
Pentagon, 40
Personal dignity, 11
Personnel assignment problems, 70
Personnel director, HQMC, 62
Physical fitness, xi, 2
Physical training, 24, 57, 66–67, 92, 94
Pith helmet, 60, 72
Platoon 71, 31–34, 37, 61, 83
Platoon guidon, 68
Platoon sergeant, 30
"Police duty," 78
Political indoctrination, 89, 91
Prayer at recruits' meals, 91
Press conference, 41, 44–45, 50
Press releases, 39, 47, 107
Pretrial Investigations, 95, 105
Price, Bem, 15, 63–64, 103, 105–110
Primary groups, 6, 8
Prisoners of war, xi
Procedures Analysis Branch, HQMC, 62
Profanity, use of, 15, 17–18, 24
Promotion policies, 50
Protocol, congressional, 47
Public Affairs Officer, 104
Public affairs, 3, 50, 61, 101–103, 107, 110
Pugil-stick fights, 102

Puller, Lt. Gen. Lewis B., 74, 83–84

Quantico, Va., 29, 45, 115
Quartermaster sergeant, 10
Questionnaires, 62, 63
Quonset huts, 24

Racial prejudice, 26–27
Radio broadcasts, 43
Receiving barracks, 71
Recovery efforts, 43, 44
Recreation facilities, 98
Recreation, Parris Island area, 24
Recruit Training Command, 49, 56,
    60–61, 65–66, 70, 72, 87, 89, 100–101,
    111; principal staff officers, 57
Recruit Training Regiment, 6, 111
Recruit sentries, 33–34, 37
Recruit training history, 10, 12
Reform measures, 3, 59
Relief for cause, 53, 108
Relief of B. Gen. Greene, 108–110
Replacement system, 7, 8
Retirement policies, 32, 119
Ribbon Creek, xi, xiv, 1, 4, 9, 12, 18,
    25, 27, 29, 34, 35, 36–38, 43, 53, 121
Ribbon Creek formula for recruit
    training crises, 112
Ribbon Creek incident, 41, 46, 48, 73,
    83, 86, 92, 100, 111–112, 115, 118
Ridgely, Maj. Gen. Reginald H., 58
Rifle company, 6
Rifle platoon, 7
Rifle qualification rates, 92–93
Rifle range, 6, 13, 31, 33–35, 37, 92
Rites of passage, 5, 112
Roberts, B. Gen. Carson A., 40
Rookie squads, 10
Roosevelt, President Franklin D., 16
Russell, Sen. Richard B., 41, 52

Saipan, Mariana Islands, 8, 62
Saltonstall, Sen. Leverett, 41
San Diego, Calif., 6, 12–13, 54, 71, 92,
    116
Sand fleas, 11, 13–14
Scarborough, T. Sgt. Elwyn B., 33, 51
Schatzel, Col. DeWolf, 48
"Sea stories" by recruit graduates, 19
Second New Look Policy, 69
Secretary of the Navy, 51–52, 77–78,
    85, 108
Selection boards, 32, 120

Senate Armed Services Committee,
    41–42, 47–48
Senate Internal Security Subcommittee,
    106, 108
Series system, institution of, 99
Sevier, Maj. Charles B., 78, 83, 85
Shapley, B. Gen. (later Lt. Gen.) Alan,
    54, 71, 116
Shaw, B. Gen. Samuel R., xiv, 11,
    40–41, 45–46, 54, 82
Shaw, Henry I., Jr., xiii
Shepherd, Gen. Lemuel C., 19
Shock treatment, 3, 94, 111
Shor, Toots, 86
Short, Rep. Dewey, 41, 52
Shoup, Gen. David M., 45, 54, 60–62,
    65, 67, 69, 71, 83, 98–101, 115,
    120–121
Shulimson, Jack, xiii, xiv
Silverthorn, Lt. Gen. Merwin H.,
    19–21, 113–114
Simmons, B. Gen. Edwin H., xiii
Simpson, Lt. Gen. Ormond R., 45, 78,
    82
Sirhan Sirhan, 120
Skinhead haircut, 61
Small-unit leadership, 7
Smart, Robert W., 52–53
Smith, Maj. Richard A., 12–14
Snedeker, Maj. Gen. Edward F., 70, 97
Social science research, 6, 8
Socialization of Marines, 118
South Carolina legislature, 102–103
Spatial dispersion of units, 8
Special Training Branch, 2
Special Training Company, 67–68, 71
Special court-martial, 20. *See also*
    Courts-martial
Special instructor sections, 17
Squadbay, 34, 37
Staff NCO Advisory Council, 59–60, 93
Staff responsibilities, 19
Standard problems of recruit training,
    104
Status of noncommissioned officers,
    114
Stealing from recruits, 14
Stefano, Charles J., 75
Stetson (J. B. Stetson Hat Company),
    72
Strother, Regina, xiii
Sullivan, Lt. Col. Richard L., 63
Summary court-martial, 20, 95. *See
    also* Courts-martial

Supervision, 25, 31, 33, 72
Survey of Recruit Training, 18–19, 62
Swagger stick, 16, 27
Swamps. *See* Tidal marsh

Tarawa, 54, 112
Telephone company, Beaufort, S.C., 43
Teletype, 38
"The Caine Mutiny," 86
Thomas, Capt. F. S., 90
Thomas, Secretary of the Navy Charles
  S., 77
Thomason, John W., Jr. 10
Tidal marsh, 34–35, 44, 51
Tidal streams, 51
Tides, 35
To Keep Our Honor Clean (novel by
  Edwin McDowell), 114
"Today" television show, 76–77
Tombstone promotions, 32, 120
Totalitarianism, instruction about, 91
Training incentives, 68
Training initiatives, 97
Transport aircraft, 58, 72, 102
Trench systems, 8
Trope, S. Sgt. William S., 20, 25
Trout hole, 35
Tshirgi, Col. Harvey C., 80
Turtinan, Ralph, 16
Twining, Gen. Merrill H., xiv, 45,
  47–56, 77, 85, 115–116

UCMJ. *See* Uniform Code of Military
  Justice
Unannounced inspections, 13
Undesirable discharge, 23
Uniform Code of Military Justice
  (UCMJ), 4, 22–24, 51, 76, 80, 94–95,
  114
Uniforms, 62
Unit cohesion, 6–8

United Press International, 43
Unlimited free laundry policy for DIs,
  71
U.S. Army, 8, 26, 33, 63
U.S. Marine Corps units: 1st Marine
  Division, 7, 9, 32, 46, 99, 104; 1st
  Recruit Training Battalion, Parris
  Island, 31; 2d Marine Division 50, 57,
  62; 4th Marines, 62
U.S. Naval Academy, 45, 51, 58, 70
U.S. Naval Institute *Proceedings*, 90
U.S. Navy, 10, 47
U.S. Senate, 48
USS Essex, 30

Vance, Col. Robert T., 57–58, 95
Vertical envelopment doctrine, 46
Veterans, 7, 33
Veterans' meetings for McKeon's
  defense, 75
Veterans Administration, 119, 121
Vietnam War, 6–7, 103, 110
Vinson, Rep. Carl, 41, 47–49, 52–53
Virginia Military Institute, 40, 119
Voluntary enlistments, 90

Washington, D.C., 40, 46, 50–51, 62,
  75, 78, 87, 108
"Watching television" (punishment), 24
Watergate Affair, 1, 103
Weapons Training Battalion, 26, 32,
  37–38, 44, 57, 92
Wheelwright, 1st Lt. Neil S., 66
Williams, Col. James R., xiii
Wood, Capt. Ralph C., 42
Wood, Charles A., xiii
Wood, Pvt. Norman, 36
World War I, 10–11
World War II, 1, 4, 7, 9, 14–15, 17, 23,
  30, 32, 42, 54, 60, 62, 103, 112

Zola, Emile, 71